The Need
to Believe

MURDO EWEN
MACDONALD

COLLINS

fontana books

First published 1959

CONTENTS

CHAPTER I

AGE OF ANXIETY

IN THE year 627 A.D., Edwin, King of Northumbria, pressed hard by the missionary Paulinus, was in two minds whether to accept Christianity or not. He called a council of his wise men and asked them what they thought of this new faith. Coifi, the head of the heathen priests, spoke in cynical vein. In the silence that followed, one of the warriors addressed the company in the now famous words :

" The present life of man upon earth, O King, seems to me in comparison with that land which is unknown to us, like to the swift flight of a sparrow through that house wherein you sit at supper in winter, with your ealdormen and thegns, while the fire blazes in the midst and the hall is warmed, but the winter storms of rain or snow are raging abroad. The sparrow flying in at one door and immediately out at another, whilst he is within safe from the wintry tempest, but after a short space of fair weather he immediately vanishes out of your sight, passing from winter into winter again, so this life of man appears for a little while, but of what is to follow or what went before, we know nothing at all. If therefore this new doctrine tells us something more certain, it seems justly to deserve to be followed."

This moving utterance proved decisive. It persuaded Edwin to accept the Christian faith, a decision which was to have consequences of incalculable significance. The unknown warrior must have been a man of uncanny perception, for throughout his speech he skilfully played on man's inborn sense of insecurity in a world full of

danger and uncertainty. Because he stands facing dark
uncharted regions that lie beyond his ken, he is not so
ready to dismiss answers which claim to cast a measure
of light upon the ultimate mystery.

There can be no denying that many of our fears have
receded as modern man has attained an increasing control over the forces of Nature. But paradoxically enough
the more powerful the telescope through which we peer
into outer space, or the more revealing the microscope
with which we examine infinitesimal particles of matter,
the deeper the mystery grows. It is open to question
whether science has made any difference to the essential human situation. We are no more at home in this
world of man-made satellites than these Anglo Saxon
thanes were, shivering in the winter cold of ancient
Northumbria. This, as Auden says, is an age of anxiety.
" Mankind ", writes Lewis Mumford, " is afloat on a
frail life raft. Religion understands the mysteries of the
deep and the storms that come up in the night."

The chronic sense of anxiety characteristic of the
human race at all stages of its development can be
seen in the sphere of international politics. Political pacts like the Atlantic Alliance or the Baghdad
Treaty, and the creation of an organisation like the
United Nations are all expressions of universal tension.
Political leaders of all countries, themselves the victims
of fears and suspicions, bluster and threaten and confuse vital issues. All this exacerbates rather than lessens
international unrest. The atom bomb was the concrete
outward symbol of our deep underlying dread. Its re-
placement by the hydrogen bomb has only emphasised
Christ's warning that Satan cannot cast out Satan,[1]
and that fear contains within itself the seeds of violence
and destruction. The latest competitive race for the
control of outer space is but another indication, if any

[1]Mark 3, v. 23 and 26; Luke 11, v. 18.

is needed, that our basic sense of insecurity is assuming cosmic dimensions.

We meet this same anxiety on the social level too. When William Wilberforce was fighting for the emancipation of slaves and Lord Shaftesbury was battling in the House of Commons to reduce the working hours of women and children, the economic and social condition of the <u>proletariat</u> was pitiful beyond description. *Labour ing classes* The mass of social legislation in existence to-day regulating work and leisure and protecting the individual from ruthless exploitation, assuring him of unemployment benefit and adequate medical care in illness, is the answer of society to the chill feeling of uncertainty that once gnawed at its vitals.

Most of all, anxiety makes itself felt on the personal level. That is by no means a phenomenon resulting from the complexities of a mechanical age. John Bunyan, George Fox, and Soren Kierkegaard who lived in more tranquil times would be called victims of anxiety neurosis by psychologists to-day. Every passing age has produced its crop of Hamlets, morbidly <u>introvertive,</u> hyper- *to turn inward* sensitive, over-wrought, contemplating suicide and crying :

> *The time is out of joint. O cursed spite,*
> *That ever I was born to set it right.*

This is true, but anxiety to-day is perhaps more prevalent than it has ever been before. If more people are afraid it is because they possess the apparatus of fear to a greater degree than ever before. If more people are corroded with guilt it is because conscience has been tampered with more effectively than at any other time. If more people are plagued by a sense of meaninglessness, it is because fewer meanings have been left unmolested.

Anxiety on the political, social, and individual levels

can, in the end, result in neurosis, psychosis, or even insanity. Every tenth bed in our hospitals is occupied by the mentally ill, and although revolutionary strides have been made in the treatment of patients with the newest and latest drugs, yet because of the pressures of a maddeningly complex society can we scarcely cope with the numbers. Nervous breakdown is common. Within the last thirty years the psychiatrist has attained a position of immense prestige. To thousands upon thousands of despairing souls he holds out a ray of hope and the promise of emotional stability. Among many sections of educated people he has successfully supplanted the minister of religion as a medium of salvation.

There is, however, a large class of society which does not fall into the category of either the neurotic or the mentally ill, yet lives constantly under the shadow of anxiety. Arthur Koestler, who is certainly no puritan, describes this feeling in his autobiographical *Arrow in the Blue*. " This latent apprehension, the awareness of guilt and impending punishment, seemed to be always present, like the rhythmic beat of the surf at night along the shore. While there are voices under the open window and laughter on the pier one is able to forget it, but when the laughter dies away and voices are stilled, the muffled thunder swells up again and one realises that it has always been present, and that the waves will never stop beating their heads against the stones of the pier."

But a more fundamental question thrusts itself to the forefront. What is the nature of anxiety? Why should it be an innate characteristic of man at every succeeding stage of his development? Why is it such an ubiquitous and inescapable fact?

To begin to answer that question we must first of all distinguish anxiety from fear. The object of fear is something concrete to which we can give a definite name. A man may be afraid to jump out of an aeroplane because the available statistics point to an element of risk and uncertainty, or he may be afraid of the secret police because some of his friends have either mysteriously disappeared, or been cruelly liquidated. Or, he may be like the curé in *The Diary of a Country Priest,* afraid of a pain in his stomach, because he suspects it is cancer. Fear always has reference to some known object and takes the form of flight from it.

Anxiety on the other hand is very different. It is not something we can put our finger on. It is a mood that fluctuates in its intensity, yet is curiously pervasive and persistent, and flight from it takes the form, not of escape, but of a more thorough-going preoccupation with the world. A man like Augustine prior to his conversion, sought to escape this sense of impending calamity by a furious concentration on the sensual, but it only sharpened his sense of inner restlessless and deepened his feeling of dread.

The modern philosopher, Martin Heidegger, writing from a non-Christian and a non-theistic point of view, claims that the meaning of anxiety is the disclosure of the self pitched into a hostile world, coupled with the consciousness that he is not at home therein. This analysis touches the very threshold of religion. Man's sense of inner disquiet, his basic restlessness, his inability to feel at home within the most congenial environment, points beyond himself to something pressing in on him from outside. We are permanently anxious in this world, because in the language of the New Testament we are " strangers and pilgrims ".[1] Our illusory sense of complacency and contentment is shattered because our lives have no real meaning apart from the God Who created us.

Paul Tillich, the theologian, in his book *The Courage to Be,* draws a clear distinction between what he calls

[1] I Peter 2, v. 11.

pathological and existential anxiety. The pathological victim needs the help of the skilled psychiatrist, whereas the normal kind of anxiety in which we all share, must look for help not in the direction of medicine but of religion. According to Tillich, in the normal form of anxiety there are present, no matter how well hidden, three dominant elements. First, there is a sense of blank meaninglessness from which the soul of man recoils in horror. Even the professional sceptics who have long since bidden good-bye to the God of orthodoxy, have spent strenuous years trying to discern some cosmic plan or intelligence behind the flux and flow of phenomena. No man is happy in the belief that life is at the mercy of blind chance. Second, there is a deep ineradicable sense of guilt in human nature to which all great literature of the world bears witness. It issues in a feeling of foreboding and suppressed apprehension. Perhaps Coleridge was talking from personal experience when he makes the Ancient Mariner say:

> *Like one that on a lonesome road*
> *Doth walk in fear and dread,*
> *And having once turned round, walks on,*
> *And turns no more his head;*
> *Because he knows a frightful fiend*
> *Doth close behind him tread.*

Third, there is the fear of death. We are not as preoccupied with the brevity of life as our fathers were. Not so many sermons are preached on this theme, but underneath our careless devil-may-care attitudes this latent dread lurks, conditioning not only our individual behaviour but also our everyday social conventions. The common practice among doctors of concealing from a dying man the fact of his impending death is evidence of this. Here is the basic anxiety, the fear that the Ego,

(1) Pathology - Science of the nature, causes, and remedies of diseases.

with all its accomplishments and potentialities, will suffer
final extinction.

In a German prison camp I remember an officer coming to me in a state of great distress. He had convinced
himself that the Gestapo had planned a mass extermination of all prisoners of war and that he would never
see his friends again. I tried to help him by ridiculing
his fears and appealing to his common sense, but the
harder I tried the more nervous he became. Then one
day I was told that as a fighter pilot he had shot down
seventeen enemy planes. When I heard this I realised
that the man was very far from being a physical coward
and that he must be hiding something which was the
real cause of his distress. I put it to him bluntly that
if he wanted my help he would have to be absolutely
honest with me. Then he decided to speak, and told me
a most tragic story of sin and bitter remorse. The
memory of what he had done gave him no peace and
tension increased until his anxiety had reached pathological proportions. It took a long time before he was
convinced that he could only find relief for his distress
of mind and anxiety of soul in forgiveness and reconciliation and a saving sense of God.

Augustine knew the meaning of anxiety and no one
has analysed it more profoundly than he did in his
Confessions. But after his conversion, he came to know
the peace that God alone can give, and could therefore
write :

" Thou hast formed us in Thine own Image, and our
hearts are restless till they find rest in Thee."

CHAPTER 2

IMPACT OF SCIENCE

To GRASP the sharpness of the conflict between religion and science in the last century, we have only to read the biographies of Charles Darwin and Henry Drummond. The one was a scientist of the first magnitude, the other a brilliant populariser who could take the discoveries of profounder minds and express them in language the ordinary man could understand. Drummond's book, *Natural Law in the Spiritual World* first delivered as lectures to working class audiences in Glasgow, became a best-seller. Its success showed that in the second half of the nineteenth century the clash between faith and reason excited not merely the intellectual but also the man in the street.

To-day we live in a very different atmosphere. The accent is no longer on rift, but on reconciliation. The sharp edge of controversy has been smoothed by a new spirit.

The reason for the change is two-fold. Religion, having learned from bitter experience, has shed some of its cast-iron dogmatism. In the past it lost considerable prestige and not a little power in its attempt to throttle the spirit of free enquiry and impede the irresistible advance of knowledge. It now recognises that Truth cannot be equated with any one system of orthodoxy. There is a wide-spread realisation among theologians that religion must rather build on a rock against which the waves of clashing theories and the tide of conflicting discoveries will dash themselves in vain.

A similar approach is evident in scientific circles.

14

equated – To reduce to an average or to a standard of comparison.

Scientists are now more ready to admit that there are vast tracts of human experience not amenable to their method. When we hear men of the calibre of Professor Eddington declare that materialism is out of date since no one knows what "matter" is, and Professor Whitehead state that there are no natural laws, only temporary habits of nature, we begin to glimpse a little of the new humility which has displaced the old exclusive attitude.

Does this mean, then, that the conflict is at an end, that the issue is settled, that the divorced parties have come together to live happily and harmoniously under the same roof? Such optimism would be unwarranted and would destroy the tension that must inevitably exist between faith and reason. Human behaviour is not always ruled by logic. A man's philosophy of life is compounded of many elements, among which the irrational is well to the fore. He may be fully aware of the fact that the chasm once thought to be impassable is now in process of being bridged, but his whole outlook may nevertheless be dominated and determined by the prevailing psychological climate.

Science can never disprove God. In a universe so vast, so complex, so utterly mysterious, we can safely rule out any such contingency, but its values may so infect our thinking, and its spirit may so permeate the fabric of our society that in time the world of faith will begin to lose its meaning and relevance. The scientific impact of the last few centuries has set in motion powerful repercussions that reach out to the uttermost bounds of human thinking.

One major consequence of this revolution is that God has become increasingly remote. Before the mediaeval cosmology was shattered by the emergence of modern science, this earth was thought to be at the centre of God's providential care. Earthquakes and floods and volcanoes might from time to time raise awkward questions, but they did not shake the conviction that this little planet was the special object of divine solicitude. It was supported and sustained by the strong everlasting arms of the Almighty.

Copernicus, in 1543, published his famous *De Revolutionibus Orbium* in which he claimed that the earth, far from remaining motionless at the centre, actually travelled round the sun. The full implications of this theory were not grasped at once, but from the start it became crystal clear that this little planet on which we mortals dwell was robbed of its position of unique and unrivalled importance.

In 1687, in his *Principia,* Newton communicated to the world his startling discoveries. The times, the position of the heavenly bodies, and their movement through space, could be adequately explained by the law of gravitation. God only intervened when something went wrong with the cosmic machinery. Newton himself, a simple devout Christian, could not possibly foresee the far-reaching consequences of this revolutionary theory on future generations.

When the epoch-making book, Darwin's *Origin of Species* appeared in 1859, orthodoxy again received a severe shock. In his book, Darwin argued that man was not created at a comparatively recent date such as 6000 B.C., but evolved gradually through a slow painful process over millions of years. It is difficult for us, who from our infancy have used the word " evolution ", to grasp how this theory convulsed Victorian thinking to its inner core.

Came the branch of science we call astro-physics. It immeasurably extended our horizons, revealing countless universes, innumerable multitudes of planets, mysterious nebulae, incredible distances computed in light years, and in comparison it reduced this earth to an infinitesimal size, like one solitary leaf in a vast forest, or a single grain of sand on the seashore.

It is true, of course, that not one of these discoveries affects in the slightest the validity of religion, but they have done something drastic to our human thinking. They have not disproved God, but they have elbowed Him out from the centre of human consciousness. Secure in the knowledge that we live in a law-abiding universe where the vast majority of events are predictable and even ascertainable, God is pushed out to the very circumference of things and is only called upon when the clockwork of normal events does not function. That is why for the ordinary man to-day religion is a last ditch recourse, something he turns to in desperation when nothing else offers him any hope.

Another important consequence of the rise of science is that, for many people, God becomes less and less essential. There was a time when religion was believed to bestow special favours on those who fulfilled certain conditions. This clearly emerges in the Old Testament. Moses, fleeing before the pursuing Egyptians, finds the Red Sea miraculously divided for him at the critical moment. The starving children of Israel are fed with manna from heaven. Jacob is blessed with numerous children and fat herds of cattle because he struck a shrewd bargain with the Almighty. However shocked we may feel by this, it is clear that these men believed religion could meet their various needs and supply their material wants.

Now it is precisely at this point that science confronts us with its sharpest challenge. On the intellectual plane its influence is impressive enough, but on a practical level it is simply overwhelming. It has ridiculed our stupidest superstitions and stretched beyond measure our cramped horizons. It has increased our leisure, our standard of living, our means of enjoyment. It has dazzled us with its scintillating successes.

Science has learned to harness the powers of nature to human use. In former days, when droughts spelt death for millions, men stormed heaven with their prayers in vain. Now-a-days, we know that irrigation, not prayer, is the answer to the problem. In Australia men no longer pray for water. They build hydro-electric plants and carry it thousands of miles through pipes. The ancient dream has come true. " The wilderness and the solitary place shall be glad . . . and the desert shall rejoice, and blossom as the rose."[1]

The same is more or less true of disease. In mediaeval times, plagues and pestilences decimating entire populations were regarded as visitations of an angry deity. We know now that they were due to septic drains and faulty hygiene. Science has by no means mastered all disease, but it has to a remarkable degree alleviated the pangs of pain and suffering. It has also conquered space through the media of aeroplane, radio and television, so that in a very real sense we are living in one world. It is not surprising therefore to find so many who claim that whereas science deals with the rational and the measurable, religion preoccupies itself with the romantic and the mystical.

The Christian, while giving full credit to all these magnificent achievements, must ask the scientific humanist to keep two facts in mind. The first is that science, far from diminishing the mysteries of the Universe, has in actual fact increased them. The second is that science can only proceed on certain assumptions which are indistinguishable from faith. It is forced to assume the rationality of the universe and the competence of the human mind to correlate the available evidence and to draw therefrom the correct conclusions.

But it is when we examine the sphere of the distinctively human that we begin to see the tragic limitations of science. The inner core of our human existence, where we are most fully and most wholly ourselves,

[1]Isaiah 35, v. 1.

is the personal. This must never be equated with the merely "individual", "private" and "solitary". The personal life may have rhythms of withdrawal and return, withdrawal into solitariness and return to contact and communication, but essentially it is one of human relationships including our families and our friendships. If a man fails in his personal life his most brilliant successes in public life will not make up for it. If the failure is serious and tragic as it often is, the past must be blotted out, and a new beginning must be made. He must become reconciled with those he has wronged and with the moral censor within himself, else there is no inner peace and no sense of wholesomeness in any of his activities. To describe such a human dilemma we must use not the symbols and formulae of science but words like "love", "forgiveness", "renewal", which are so natural to religion.

Over against the abstract laws of science stands the God of the Bible Who is intensely personal and accessible. Even in the Old Testament the sense of divine imminence is sometimes very vivid. We find the Psalmist overwhelmed with this consciousness, crying "Whither shall I go from Thy Spirit? or whither shall I flee from Thy Presence?[1] If I ascend up into Heaven, Thou art there : if I make my bed in hell, behold, Thou art there. If I take the wings of the morning and dwell in the uttermost parts of the sea; even there shall Thy hand lead me, and Thy right hand shall hold me." And the God of the New Testament is even more accessible. Jesus did not pray to a First Cause or a Cosmic Abstraction. He prayed to a Father Who not only hears but also answers. "Ask, and it shall be given you; seek, and ye shall find; knock and it shall be opened unto you."[2] In Sir Walter Scott's *Heart of Midlothian,* there is a moving scene where Jeanie Deans set off to London to plead in person with the Queen for the life of

[1]Ps. 139, v. 7 to 10. [2]Matt. 7, v. 7; Luke 11, v. 9.

her condemned sister. Reuben Butler, the schoolmaster, tried his best to dissuade her. "London is a long distance away; the road is infested with robbers, and you are only a woman," he pleaded. "Why not send a letter?" And Jeannie answered—"Writing wouldna' do it. A letter canna look and pray and beg and beseech as a human voice can do to the human heart. A letter's like the music that the ladies have for their spinets— nothing but black scores compared with the same tune played and sung. The word of mouth maun do it, or naething else." If the inner throbbing core of our human existence is the personal, then we must look not to science but to religion for the answer.

In conclusion, the limitation of science is seen most clearly in its inability to generate power on a moral level. It cannot lift a single defeated soul out of the abyss of self-loathing and despair, but where science dismally fails, religion dynamically succeeds. To doubt this is to dismiss the saints and mystics as victims of fantasy and self-deception. Tolstoy was a man of genius and at the same time a slave to sensuality. He could write imperishable literature, but he could not curb his animal passions. In the end he was liberated, not by science but by faith. "Five years ago I came to believe in Christ's teaching, and my life suddenly became changed. I ceased desiring what I had wished for before. The direction of my life, my desires, became different. What was good and bad changed places."

If science has mesmerised our age by its miracles of practical achievements, it cannot be too strongly stressed that in the arena of our deepest and most desperate need it has done nothing for us. That is why religion is never out of date and why it speaks just as cogently to our space-minded generation as it did to Abraham when he struck his tents in Ur of the Chaldees long ago. The New Testament from beginning to end is pre-occupied not with a God Who is becoming increasingly more remote and progressively less and less essential in the struggle of life, but with a mighty Saviour whose resources are always available, and in every crisis more than adequate. If Christianity were to have a signature tune, it would surely be " Christ is able ". " Wherefore, He is able to save them to the uttermost ", says the author of the Epistle to the Hebrews.[1] " Now unto Him that is able to keep you from falling, and to present you faultless before the presence of His glory with exceeding joy ",[2] is the concluding word of the epistle of Jude. " Now unto Him that is able to do exceeding abundantly above all that we ask or think ",[3] cries Paul in a passionate lyrical outburst. Faith, not science, is the power of God unto salvation.

[1] Hebs. 7, v. 25.   [2] Jude, v. 24.   [3] Ephesians 3, v. 20.

CHAPTER 3

QUESTION OF PSYCHOLOGY

LESS THAN one century old, Psychology has come to exercise an influence on modern life we can no longer ignore. It permeates the whole of our every day existence, our work and play, our reactions to the world around us, and our attitude to God and man. The more complex and intimate the human situation, the stronger its grip grows and the more resounding is its authority.

To begin with Psychology had to fight hard for recognition. The orthodox sciences and the established professions looked askance at what they regarded as a freakish development. Superciliously they alleged it would only appeal to the eccentric fringe, and that after time had unmasked its absurd pretensions, it would sink back into the limbo of discredited superstitions.

These confident predictions have proved false. Psychology has now such a strong position in society that no amount of denigration can dislodge it. Most universities, in the western world at least, have installed a chair on the subject. The sale of literature on the subject far outstrips that of theology and philosophy, and words like "complex", "inhibition" and "neurosis" have become part of our normal vocabulary.

Psychology has gained for itself a firm foothold in medicine. The fact that many of the great psychologists like William James, Siegmund Freud and Carl Jung were qualified doctors is significant. The psychologist has become such a familiar figure in our society that he is now prominent on the contemporary stage, and in the pages of *Punch* and the *New Yorker*. His universal acceptance is due to an ever-growing recognition on the part of doctors that there are more things in heaven and earth than are dreamt of in their physiology. The psychiatrist, while recognising that the psychological factor forms only one pole of the psychic cosmos, often in practice uses the concepts and methods of the psycho-analyst.

Psychology has also penetrated industry to considerable depth. Its application to practical problems of efficiency and production is fast becoming one of its chief occupations. The industrial psychologist has largely succeeded in convincing the hard-headed business man that the element of fatigue, physical and mental, affects productivity in no small measure. He has proved that the average worker will get as much done in fifty-four hours a week as he will in sixty to seventy hours. He has also shown that though a good wage is an incentive, it is by no means the crucial factor. Loyalty cannot be bought by canteen facilities or handsome bonuses. What counts in the long run is the mutual respect of employer and employee. The technique of teaching management how best to co-operate with labour is becoming a major preoccupation.

Another field in which Psychology has made itself felt is education. Human beings are born without the complex built-in pattern of instincts which make salmon swim up stream to spawn and birds migrate thousands of miles with uncanny accuracy. Man has to learn practically everything he knows, and Psychology has shed much light on the processes of memory, association and the correlation of ideas. The Intelligence Test —a measurement of man's ability to learn—is an invention of the psychologist. The initials I.Q. are only too well known, though perhaps not everyone knows what the term means, and though it may not be as infallible a guide as some people are disposed to believe.

The most recent use of Psychology is in the realm of advertisement. It has been known for a long time that people are prompted by motives of which they are completely unconscious, so a technique has emerged called "motivation research". The idea is to learn the real motives that determine human behaviour and to harness the process of advertising on to them. This practice seems to lend substance to the view held in certain quarters that Psychology is a dark and infamous cult which in the hands of the unscrupulous can reduce man to the level of a mechanical robot. In fairness, however, it should be stressed that on this whole issue there is a sharp division of opinion among the psychologists themselves.

It is abundantly clear, then, that Psychology is a force to be reckoned with in the twentieth century. Its influence is all-pervasive—some would say all-powerful —in our society and so we are faced with the problem of evaluation. Where does it stand in relation to religion? Is it the sworn enemy of theology, sabotaging its foundations, or is it a staunch ally, helping it in the desperately difficult task of human redemption. In considering this important question, we must be on our guard against two common errors which tend to confuse the issue and to result in a hopeless ambiguity.

The first error is that of Psychologism. It is committed by those psychologists who go beyond the boundaries of their own science and dogmatise on questions which belong to the realm of philosophy and religion. Freud was a notorious sinner in this respect. As a psychologist his genius is beyond dispute, but he was a poor philosopher lacking the temperament and proper equipment for such a study. When he talks of complex inhibition or neurosis he must be taken seriously for he was a man of profound insight, but when he denounces religion as illusion he is propounding conclusions not based on psychological investigation but on naïve philosophical presuppositions he had neither formulated nor brought to the bar of rational criticism. There are definite limits to the study of scientific psychology. Professor John MacMurray makes this clear in his book *The Boundaries of Science*. He writes : " It is at once true that all human behaviour can be investigated scientifically, that there is no human activity which is excluded from the field of scientific psychology, and also that there is one aspect of human behaviour which must necessarily escape completely from the account that science gives. And it is indeed precisely this aspect which makes human behaviour specifically human." The important thing to remember is that the psychologist can only talk authoritatively on the analysis, classification, and to a limited degree on the interpretation of religious experience. On the objective reality which is the ultimate source of that subjective experience, he can say nothing at all.

The second error is Theologism, which flourishes not only in a certain type of preaching, but also in professional academic circles. It arose out of a strong reaction against the sort of liberalism which understated the seriousness of man's predicament and exaggerated the saving potency of human knowledge. When this naïve liberalism collapsed before the savage onslaught of totalitarian man, a " crisis theology " emerged which seemed to place an exclusive emphasis on God's power to redeem and to deny man even the capacity to respond. It is true that there is a wide range of emphases among those who belong to this school, but the extremists would welcome a head-on collision between theology and other branches of human knowledge. Man, they say, is a swaggering Titan who openly defies God and he cannot be lured to a saving knowledge of Him along the paths of sweet reasonableness.

The result is that certain theologians and preachers have retreated to their ivory towers, cells and catacombs. They are suspicious of modern culture and regard Psychology as a particularly heinous expression of humanism. They rest content with preaching what they call the prophetic Word, and leave the psychotherapist to wrestle with tormented souls in the grip of desperate neurosis, wondering if there is any release from bondage.

The wise man will repudiate the twin errors of Psychologism and Theologism, but he will be equally suspicious of any self-conscious synthesis that would lead to a process of abstraction every bit as unrelated to the human dilemma. What he will in fact seek is a reconciliation of the old antitheses, a healing of the old dualisms, an increasing readiness for co-operation on the part of theologians and psychotherapists resulting in a more thorough going integration of life and experience. The psychotherapist as he inevitably sheds the immaturities of a new science, is beginning to see that the insights of theology are vindicated by his clinical discoveries. No matter what the difficulties are on a theoretical level, there are certain practical problems where co-operation between the two disciplines is not merely desirable but absolutely imperative.

One such problem is sin. Whatever modern label we stick on to it—complex, neurosis or fixation, it reveals itself in what the New Testament calls bondage. Whatever explanation we advance for its existence—evolutionary lag, social maladjustment, or ignorance—the result is ever the same, an abject enslavement of the will. Whatever the causes that produce it, they are so inwrought into human nature that all our strivings seem destined to defeat. Paul was not romanticising, he was voicing the despair of all humanity when he cried : " O wretched man that I am ! who shall deliver me from the body of this death ?"[1]

Nor do the psychologists draw a pretty picture of human nature. Freud was no theologian, but he claimed to have discovered in the dark recesses of man's unconsciousness what he called the " id ", and by the " id "

[1]Romans 7, v. 24.

he meant a riotous kingdom of selfish drives, pugnacious
urges, sensual impulses, which the Ego and super-Ego
were powerless to control. It is as if some one were
suddenly to lift the stone of our normal inhibitions only
to discover a population of ugly insects seething underneath and scuttling back to their dark holes. There
is a sense, therefore, in which modern psychology en-
dorses the classical Christian doctrine of original sin.
And the recent concept of the " collective unconscious "
only confirms the New Testament claim of the solidarity
of evil enveloping all humanity and infecting the whole
of life. The theologian while he stresses the objective
reality of sin, cosmic in the dimension and demonic in its
power, must be prepared also to accept the empirical
help of the psychotherapist as he deals with sin's ramifi-
cations in the delicate and complex structure of personality.

Another problem is what the late D. M. Baillie
calls the moral failure complex. Modern man may
may not be burdened by a sense of sin. He may have a
complacent conscience, and appear to the world blasé
and unconcerned, but underneath the blustering confidence he knows something is wrong. All men who are
not complete moral perverts, are dimly aware of this,
and when the intermittent pressure increases into an
intolerable inner tension, they turn to either psychology
or religion for an answer. It is this haunting consciousness of having failed in life that makes the young
poetess, Celia Copplestone, in T. S. Eliot's play, go to
the psychiatrist :

It's not the feeling of anything I've ever done,
Which I might get away from or of anything in me
I could get rid of, but of emptiness, of failure
Towards some one or something outside of myself,
And I feel I must atone—is that the word?
Can you treat a patient for such a state of mind?

There are various ways by which modern man tries to deal with this brutal fact of moral failure. There is the method of redefinition. He calls it complex or neurosis, believing the new label makes it easier to live with; but guilt cannot be treated as a product of a diseased imagination, or an illusion which can be bowed out of existence in this cavalier manner. The psychologist who tries to explain it away is separating himself not only from theology but from the great poets and dramatists; from Shakespeare as well as from Augustine, from Euripides as well as from Paul.

And there is the method of recognition. To drag the hidden festering complex up into the light of day is the remedy offered by some psychologists. To be sure certain phobias, especially those of a trivial nature can be cured in this manner, but guilt is different. It is based not on fantasy but on solid fact, and it demands a more radical treatment. If we try to cut the Gordian knot of moral failure in this way, it has the awkward knack of tying itself again. There is no answer for man's besetting dilemma, short of forgiveness. While this cannot be too strongly emphasised, it is also true that the psychotherapist's help is needed in the classifying of mental disorders and the disentangling of emotional disturbances. Here as elsewhere, the accent must be on intelligent co-operation, not mutual antagonism.

Finally there is the problem of integration which comes near to what the Bible means by salvation. The psychotherapist is faced not only with the task of diagnosing mental illness, but also with the far more difficult one of helping the patient towards a measure of integration. "It is in fact impossible," says Jung, "to treat the soul and the human personality sectionally. In all disturbances of the psyche, it is apparent that the psyche is a whole in which everything is connected with everything else."

It is possible to be a brilliant scientist and even an

outstanding psychologist and yet be overwhelmed by personal problems over which the intellect exercises no effective control. In his novel *The Genius and the Goddess,* Aldous Huxley recognises this. One of the main characters, a great mathematician, he describes as " empty, swept and garnished. Empty of God, swept clean of common manhood, and garnished with glittering notions. And seven other devils worse than stupidity and sentimentality had moved in and taken possession."

Now it is clear that if there is a God Who is active and capable of entering into what Martin Buber calls an " I—Thou " relationship, integration in the profound and permanent sense cannot take place without a recognition of His Sovereignty. If He is the ground of all existence, the One in Whom we live and move and have our being, He must be accorded a place of absolute pre-eminence before we mortals can experience the beatitude of emotional unity. This indeed is part of the meaning of the Incarnation. Jesus revealed to us One God Who demanded unconditional obedience instead of a polytheism of allegiances. It is only in communion with this God Who is also the Father of our Lord Jesus Christ, and in submission to His Holy Will that we experience the oneness which is of the very essence of salvation.

CHAPTER 4

MENACE OF SECULARISM

ASK HALF a dozen people what they understand by secularism and they will give you as many conflicting answers. The word has come to have an elastic connotation covering a wide field of varying emphases and different shades of meaning. It is not something defined, measured and calculated with any degree of scientific precision. It is a prevailing temper, a vague philosophy of life, a characteristic attitude to the world which in time has percolated down to the masses, determining their values and conditioning their everyday behaviour. Yet even if it is incapable of exact definition, it is nevertheless a threat to Christianity.

In the past there was a tendency to talk of the sacred and the secular as if they were two sharply defined distinctive realms. By the secular was meant preoccupation with the present world and its values, while the word sacred connoted what was referred to rather vaguely as the spiritual. Now it has become obvious that the rigid division has become untenable. It has resulted not only in theological heresy, but in distorted values which have been responsible for the breaking up of western civilisation. We have come to see that the sharp distinction between the sacred and the secular is neither Biblical nor Christian; it is in fact Gnostic and Manichean in origin. It is based on the false assumption that the spiritual is good while the material is evil and corrupt.

The late Archbishop of Canterbury, William Temple, did a great deal to destroy this popular fantasy. He claimed that of all the great religions of the world Christianity was by far the most materialistically minded. More than Hinduism or Mohammedanism, even more than Judaism, it concerned itself with practical humanitarianism—with, for example, prison reforms, the factory acts, the emancipation of slaves and with the alleviation of human suffering.

No Christian who takes the Incarnation seriously can ever again countenance a rigid demarcation between the realms of the sacred and the secular. God Who is Maker of heaven and earth sent Jesus Christ into the world to redeem, not only the individual soul, but the whole of society. If Lutheran pietism and Calvinistic puritanism have in the past despised the world, it is because they failed to grasp the total implications of the Word made flesh. It was the Church's failure to understand and to proclaim the fact that the earth is the Lord's and the fulness thereof which catapulted dictators like Hitler and Stalin into power. If by secularism we mean a new determination on the part of the Church to recover the lost provinces of religion and to let the Spirit of Christ interpenetrate the whole body of society, then, far from opposing it we must eagerly welcome it.

In the past, the world's greatest thinkers were subjected to bitter religious persecution. This practice was motivated by the ever-lurking fear that a new discovery on the part of science would undermine orthodox belief and discredit it in the eyes of the faithful. This negative mentality was notably illustrated by the famous "monkey trial" which took place in America as late as the twenties of this century. In one of the Southern schools a boy heard a teacher expound Darwin's theory of evolution. He went home and told his parents, who reported the matter to the appropriate educational and religious authorities. It culminated in the celebrated trial in which two famous lawyers took part. William Jennings Bryan supported the anti-evolutionists, and

Clarence Darell spoke for the Darwinians, and it all ended in the passing of anti-evolution laws in the States of Arkansas and Mississippi.

This sort of demarcation does religion great harm, but fortunately it is confined to backward communities or those subjected to ecclesiastical totalitarianism. It heavily underlines the need for absolute autonomy in the field of secular knowledge. It is almost certain that the science of medicine would not have made such striking progress in recent centuries unless it had torn itself free from the stranglehold of mediaeval theology. It had to become secular in order to lighten the burden of man's misery. The emancipation was necessary not only in medicine, but also in other fields of knowledge. "Reality", says Bishop Barry, "cannot be incarcerated in the syllogism of mediaeval theology."

With all this most modern Christians would agree; but the secularism which threatens to undermine the Christian religion is of a very different kind. It derives from the Latin word "saeculum" meaning age, and according to a recent American writer its emphasis could be described as "This ageism"—or "This is all there is ism; there isn't any more ism." Any belief in the supernatural or the after life is regarded as primitive superstition, and spiritual values are explained away as psychological projections. At the risk of over-simplifying this universal threat, subtle and complex and exceedingly difficult to define, let us consider some of its most manifest expressions in the twentieth century.

There is the philosophy of naturalism whose exponents belong to a fairly select academic circle. They are to be found on both sides of the Atlantic and although they differ to a radical degree on questions of politics and ethics they are one in placing an immoderate emphasis on the scientific approach as the only effective key to the interpretation of reality.

In America, John Dewey has been beating the

tom-tom of naturalism for well over a generation. He regards organised religion as one of the chief obstacles in the path of true progress. Values, he declares, must not be placed within the framework of theology nor must they be encumbered with the apparatus of dogmas and doctrine. They exist in their own right and their hold upon humanity is absolutely assured. In Britain, Bertrand Russell has for long been an advocate of even a more sophisticated variety of naturalism. Although he does not place such implicit faith in the omnipotence of science as Dewey, yet he would hold that in the solving of problems and the unravelling of mysteries the scientific method is superior to any other. And he is implacable in his opposition to institutional Christianity.

The Christian can only answer that though he welcomes free scientific enquiry he is opposed to the naïve naturalistic philosophy which has been superimposed upon it. He points to the Achilles heel of all naturalism, its acceptance not only of values but also of the fact that certain values are more important than others. Russell is honest enough to admit the weakness of his own position when he writes : " I find it quite intolerable to suppose that when I say cruelty is bad, I am merely saying that I do not like cruelty." Naturalism, no matter how eloquently expounded, is a bleak and barren philosophy, and it is full of inconsistencies.

Another popular expression of the secularistic spirit is humanism. The devotees of this philosophy are not necessarily anti-church like Dewey and Russell. On the contrary a surprising number of them applaud the insights and achievements of Christianity. They even confess to a wistful desire for a personal faith of which rationally speaking they are incapable. In place of the creed of a supernaturally revealed religion, they have substituted a belief in man's own natural goodness—a doctrine of self-redeemability. This is by no means a

brand new emphasis. Both Shelley and Byron proclaimed it as a high religion and the Victorian era produced its own crop of passionately eloquent prophets.

The essence of this philosophy of life lies in the fundamental assumption that faith in God is an anachronism; it is unnecessary either for the building or the
maintenance of civilisation. Man is his own saviour
and has within himself the creative and regenerative
powers which, given a reasonable chance, will refashion
society and build the new generation upon this earth.

This expression of secularism is Christianity's most
serious rival in the twentieth century. Its major defect,
however, is its blindness to the reality of evil and the
fact of human sin—the saboteurs behind the scenes;
the surd that thwarts progress all along the line. The
unpalatable truth which frustrates all self-respecting
humanists is that those who liquidated millions in
gas chambers were products of European civilisation
and culture. The men who approved the dropping
of the first atomic bomb on defenceless women and
children were not untutored savages but highly sophisticated humanists. The glorification of man does not
lead to a new heaven and a new earth, it invariably
leads to hell.

But perhaps the secularistic temper finds its com-
monest expression in idealism. Naturalism and humanism are, after all, technical philosophical terms used
and understood by the comparative few, but idealism
is something grasped and shared by the many. It is for
this reason that it can become the arch enemy of religion. There is no doubt what Dostoievsky meant when
he said humanitarianism was the most virulent form of
atheism, for with a little kindness here and a modicum
of justice there, it banished God out of His universe.

This is not to sneer at idealism which, in all conscience, is always better than cynicism; but the danger
lies in a religion which has shed the classical Christian

doctrines and the supernatural framework of Christianity, and concentrates exclusively on the ethical challenge. Jesus is divested of His cosmic stature and is no better than a Christian Confucius, a benign and lovely influence, a great historical figure, evoking respect and worthy of imitation.

It might not be unfair to claim that this is what masquerades for authentic Christianity among the majority of people to-day. Many of those who attend church zealously, promote its interests and immerse themselves in good works, have but the flimsiest hold on the fundamental beliefs without which the Church has no hope of ultimately surviving. What we are left with is Christianity without God and from this it is an easy transition to secular idealism which in time degenerates into mere idolatry.

But what is the supernatural which the naturalists scorn and the humanists blandly ignore? What content do Christians give to this word, and how do they want the ordinary person to understand it? We would not be far wrong if we were to say that they mean by it all that the Bible implies by the Creator, as distinct from the creature. This God is someone very different from Aristotle's prime mover or the cosmic spectator of the deists. He is more than the sustainer of the universe, the spring of human existence, the ground of all being. He is a Person Who revealed Himself to us in Jesus Christ, as a forgiving Father.

Christianity maintains that though such a belief may not be universally acceptable to the modern mind, it is not altogether meaningless. The words "atheism" and "agnosticism" are pregnant with that implication. It is impossible either to deny or doubt what is entirely meaningless. The Christian does not claim that he has unravelled all the mystery or that he never experiences the shock of ultimate doubt. At best he only sees through a glass darkly. What he does claim is that there is a light which shineth in the darkness, and that faith is able to pierce the shadows and apprehend it, or as T. S. Eliot has expressed it :

> For most of us, there is only the unattended
> Moment, the moment in and out of time,
> The distraction fit, lost in a shaft of sunlight,
> The wild thyme unseen, or the winter lightning,
> Or the waterfall, or music heard so deeply
> That it is not heard at all, but you are the music
> While the music lasts. These are only hints and
>   guesses,
> Hints followed by guesses; and the rest
> Is prayer, observance, discipline, thought and
>   action.
> The hint half guessed, the gift half understood is
>   Incarnation.

CHAPTER 5

ISOLATION OF RELIGION

THE WITNESS of the mediaeval Church was marred by many compromises and corruptions, but nevertheless it had effected a marvellous synthesis of all the interests and vitalities of the age. The Church presided over birth and death, and all the momentous crises in between. It dominated the horizon with walled abbeys and Gothic cathedrals. It cultivated beauty and subsidised art. It followed man into the market place and workshop. It filled the air with chant and song and prayer, and crowned the last moments of the dying with awful dignity.

But right on the heels of this prodigious achievement, one can see the process of disintegration setting in. The isolation of religion on every level of life begins to gather momentum. Bishop Barry in an illuminating passage writes: "The avowed aim of the Protestant Reformers was to set religion free from the cloister, or deliver it from its monastic exclusiveness, to establish Christian faith and piety as the inspiration of the home and market place. But in fact the results of the reforming movement have worked in almost the opposite sense. The tendency ever since the Reformation both in Roman and Reformed Churches, has been to think of religion in isolation as a self-sufficient and self-sustaining activity, torn out of that many coloured pattern of political, cultural and aesthetic interests which alone secure its vitality and wholeness."

Luther, despite his profound insight and positive achievements, seemed to lend support to the retreat of the Church from the arena of political controversy. By his stress on the inwardness of faith and the sanctity of the family, he and his followers tended to cut themselves loose from the clamorous problem of community. Lutheran pietism was a logical consequence of this particular emphasis, and beyond any doubt it paved the way for the divorce between Church and State which in time was to precipitate Hitlerism with all its satanic fury.

Calvin on the other hand believed in a theocracy. He wanted the Church not only to stand at the centre of the community, but also to regulate the economic needs and social habits of the people. The Calvinistic emphasis on work and moral discipline let loose a flood of vitality which was the driving force behind the industrial democracies of Britain and America. But despite this bold engagement with the world, it too in time began to retreat, because at its core there lurked a stark dualism between body and soul, spirit and matter.

Religion has come to be isolated politically. One has only to read a little Russian history and literature to see how much the Greek Orthodox Church used to influence the policies of the Czars and their governments; but that dubious liaison between Church and State was swept away with the Bolshevik Revolution, so that now the ruling clique feel they can afford to discount the Church as a serious force in the community. Professor Eric Ashby in his book *A Scientist in Russia* confirms this. He found no evidence of direct persecution of religion, but the Government by a deliberate policy of isolation did its best to drain it of vitality and reduce it to the level of a quaint idiosyncrasy.

It is popularly believed that whereas Protestants are in the retreat on every front, the Roman Catholic Church is strongly advancing and exercising a sinister influence on the governments of those countries where it commands a majority. Yet is it not significant that in France, Italy and Poland, all traditional strongholds of

Roman Catholicism, Communism has made its most devastating inroads? In these countries the industrial masses have strong Marxist leanings and the philosophy of atheistic existentialism has a large following among the intelligentsia. The Mother Church, for many, has become an isolated phenomenon.

In Britain, the Church is still revered, but more as a national institution than a centre of spiritual power and Christian influence. Any move in the House of Commons to suppress it would be met with the fiercest and most determined opposition, not least from those who never darken its doors. But our native tolerance of religion should not blind us to the fact that over the last few generations it has come to exercise less and less power on questions of political significance. During the general strike of 1926 a group of English Bishops tried to bring together management and labour in an attempt to end a disastrous national crisis. In the House of Commons the Prime Minister, Stanley Baldwin, made it plain that religion had no place in politics. He asked how the Bishops would like it if he referred the revision of the Athanasian Creed to the Iron & Steel Federation. The applause that greeted this sally was an eloquent reminder of the political isolation which seeks to rob religion of its prophetic function in the life of the nation.

Religion has come to be isolated socially. It can be argued that the same thing has appeared in the intellectual realm. A great many of the modern intelligentsia are spiritually disfranchised, it is true, but nevertheless the sociological isolation of the faith is a more serious matter, for the simple reason that in their everyday existence people are much more affected by social than by purely intellectual trends.

The process of isolation was given a tremendous impetus by the Industrial Revolution. We talk sometimes of the Church losing the working classes, as if this were

a recent fact, but the plain truth is that the divorce between religion and sociology began centuries ago. Langmead Casserley, in his book *The Retreat from Christianity*, supplies us with some very revealing facts on this
whole question. The growth of the City of Birmingham
helps to focus the issue and at the same time to remind
us of the tardiness of the institutional Church to take
any positive steps to cope with a rapidly changing
situation. In 1685 the population of Birmingham stood
round about 4,000. By 1760 it had risen to 29,000 and
only one church was built during that period. By 1801
the population was in the region of 74,000 but in the
interval only one more church had been erected. By
1821 it had taken a steep rise to 107,000, but only one
church had been built since 1779. This, let it be admitted, is a particularly glaring example of ecclesiastical
ineptitude, but such failures were multiplied throughout the length and breadth of the country. The industrial masses, even if they had been encouraged to
worship, had no place to go, so the prevailing social
pattern of the proletariat class became more and more
secular, not through any common choice but through
tradition and habitual acquiescence.

The real challenge to religion lies in the dehumanising
process which seems to be the inevitable by-product of
the industrial consciousness and the ascendancy of technology. The average man is so distracted by questions
of money and minimal economic security, by preoccupation with organised pleasure and canned entertainment, that he is deprived of any surplus of energy for
spiritual endeavour. "Lured by elemental needs," says
Lewis Mumford, "man tends to rest content with their
satisfaction. We have become progressively enslaved to
the machine; progressively immersed in the humdrum
of recreation; progressively addicted to synthetic satis-
factions which, however innocent and diverting they

may be in themselves, fail to invest life with any purpose or meaning."

Religion has become isolated culturally. Drama used to be controlled by the Church and in her hands was a powerful influence of evangelism, but on the heels of the Renaissance the stage began to lose this deeply spiritual impulse, and in time came to be equated for all that was lewd and libidinous in life. For this tragic development from which we are still suffering, the Church itself by its effort to superimpose an effete and bloodless Puritanism, must take a large share of the blame.

Even up to the end of the last century, the novel was the vehicle of a recognisable Christian philosophy of life. Berdyaev claims that he learned more about God from the novels of Tolstoy and Dostoievsky than from all the accepted systems of orthodox theology. In our own day it would be difficult to single out one novelist about whom a similar claim could be made. And in poetry men like Browning, Tennyson and Francis Thompson were to the fore in communicating the Christian Gospel through a medium many cultured people could read and apprehend. But to-day poetry, with the exception of a few choice spirits like T. S. Eliot and W. H. Auden, makes merely a pretence of wrestling with spiritual profundities.

When we come to art, the isolation of faith becomes even more striking. As Paul Tillich, the theologian, says : " Art indicates what the character of a spiritual situation is; it does this more immediately and directly than do science or philosophy." Modern artists, encouraged by the findings of psycho-analysis, became morbidly subjective and prophetically represented in symbol the retreat from sanity and the break up of a civilised pattern of living. Picasso, perhaps the outstanding painter of our time, portrays in practically every picture the message which grips and torments him —the drama of disintegration. Thus contemporary art, however distasteful the conventional connoisseur may find it, gives us a truer image of the modern malaise than most expressions of documentary realism do.

The problem of evangelism is a complex and formidable one. The Church is confronted not only with the task of calling individuals to repentance but with the much more difficult one of reversing the political, sociological and cultural patterns of human behaviour, which at the same time deny the reality of God and devalue the personality of man.

In such a situation the Church is always open to the temptation of becoming aggressively " this worldly ". Having been isolated for generations on end she may feel all she has to do to recover her lost prestige is to get thoroughly immersed in mundane activities. The cult of activism is an ever recurring danger and in the end it always robs religion of its depth and meaning. Such naïve strategies of advance have proved disastrous in the past, and if adopted would result in an even deeper humiliation in the future.

Still the crucial question remains—How are we to recover the surrendered territory and reclaim the lost provinces of religion? If the retreat has been going on ever since the Renaissance, how can we ever hope to stem the powerful trends, to change patterns so deeply ingrained, to cause the current of modern thought to flow in a different direction? This, in truth, is a formidable task, but it must be tackled by men of faith, even if from a human viewpoint it seems impossible.

We must seek to recover ground on the intellectual front, hence the relevance of an intelligent and robust theology. Though the primary task of the Christian Church is to declare, not to debate; to evangelise, not to apologise, there is a great need for a positive apologetic approach after the manner of Paul and Pascal. The aim of the true apologist is not to blunt the sharp edge of the Christian challenge but with that challenge to destroy man's fond illusions, to strip him of his pretences, to block every avenue of escape and to confront him in his spiritual nakedness with the totalitarian claims of the living God. The intellectual climate which conditions men's everyday thinking may have to undergo a radical change before they come to terms with the message of redemption.

We must seek to advance on the social front. In this we must not follow Rousseau and the Romanticists who sought social solutions for religious problems. We are coming to see that solitary Christianity is a contradiction in terms, that we need others in order to be ourselves, that only in community can we experience self-transcendence and enjoy freedom and fulfilment. Langmead Casserley stresses the imperative need for this approach. He writes : " The primary task of Evangelism is not to recover industrial man for God and the Church, but rather to recover him for himself. The masses must become men again if they are to hear God speak. Hence the Evangelist, however much he may desire to do so, cannot decline the mantle of the social prophet without frustrating and confounding the central purpose of his existence. To unmask the depersonalising limitations of mere industrialism, to undermine the presumptuous self-confidence of administrative, managerial, and technological types of mind—that is now an essential element in the contemporary proclamation of the Gospel."

We must advance on the aesthetic front. The true artist, be he painter, musician, poet or prose writer, possesses not only a piercing insight into the mood of the age; he also, through the medium of his art, has power to speak to the mind and conscience of his own generation. This fact emerges clearly in the poetry of W. H. Auden and T. S. Eliot; the latter in such poems as *Ash Wednesday* and *The Waste Land*; in plays like *The Confidential Clerk* and *The Cocktail Party*, portrays the dreary trivial emptiness of life without God, and speaks to a sort of sceptic the ordinary Church never reaches.

Finally, we must make a special effort to advance on the front of popular entertainment. Television is fast becoming the most powerful instrument for mass communication in the twentieth century, yet at the moment the Church has not even begun to grasp its frightening potentiality for good and evil. There are religious leaders who contemptuously dismiss it as an instrument unworthy of their attention, while all the time the values of millions of the unchurched masses are actually conditioned by it. The Church should not content herself with the traditional Sunday Service broadcast. The Church must descend from the pulpit to the arena of controversy. She should be prepared to use men of deep faith and sharp intellects to challenge brilliant exponents of modern secularism such as Julian Huxley, Bertrand Russell and A. J. Ayer. Before the eyes of watching millions, Christians ought to be able to give a reason for the hope that is in them. Television as a medium of communicating the Gospel has limitations, but it also offers unparallelled opportunities for making contact with the spectator masses. Far from belittling this modern medium, we ought to say with Paul " For a great door and effectual is opened unto me, and there are many adversaries."[1]

[1] 1st Cor., 16, 9.

CHAPTER 6

IMPORTANCE OF BELIEF

SOME YEARS ago the celebrated French philosopher, Jean-Paul Sartre, wrote a novel called *The Age of Reason*. In it he frankly records the behaviour and reactions of men and women who have discarded not only the dogmas of traditional faith but also the canons of conventional morality. Priding themselves on their complete emancipation from the normal restraints imposed by a so-called civilised society, they became firmly convinced that in everything they did, they were following the dictates of pure reason.

Sartre is not the only one who thinks that faith is a thing of the past. There are many modern thinkers who regard it as an outmoded mediaeval legacy, or a pious Victorian anachronism which has ceased to command the allegiance of intelligent people. With Matthew Arnold they feel that as the tide of knowledge rises, the sea of faith is on the ebb. It is like a clearcut mathematical formula, a simple case of inverse ratio.

This myth, for myth it is, does not bear close scrutiny. The truth is that ours is the age of belief *par excellence*, perhaps the most gullible in all history. What has happened is that traditional, time-honoured dogmas have been supplanted by other beliefs even less capable of rational proof, which demand of the individual something amounting to blind credulity.

To describe our age as superstitious rather than scientific would be much more accurate. Evidence of this abounds at every level of contemporary life. There are literally millions of people in our midst who look not to science but to astrology to forecast the future. Gambling, which has now developed into a major industry, is based on the assumption that if a man perseveres long enough his luck is bound to turn. Others in countless numbers have turned to pagan ideologies and popular philosophies. It is clear that these substitutes can offer neither *bona fide* proof nor credentials above suspicion, but nevertheless the masses are prepared to place implicit faith in them.

The Church is confronted with the task not of preaching to an age which believes in nothing but of proclaiming the gospel to a generation which has an insatiable appetite for believing the wrong things. Before we proceed to declare and press home the great basic beliefs of the faith a number of current fallacies must be exposed and demolished.

The first fallacy is that a religious creed is not really necessary. This attitude is not just characteristic of atheists who reject God in any shape or form, it is common among men and women who claim to be genuinely religious. In his book *Religion without Revelation* Julian Huxley argues that religion must not be confused with beliefs held to be supernaturally revealed. It is an attitude of mind and spirit, an emotional mood which is compatible with the most conflicting systems of theology. The significant thing about this view is not that it exists, but that it is shared by so many professedly religious people. Surprising though it may seem there are those who assure us that they can be religious without believing in God, and Christians without accepting one single doctrine of the Christian faith.

This experimental creedless religion, so characteristic of a former generation, has resulted in sorry chaos and wide-spread disillusionment. A world that has lost its bearings and has no one central belief to which it can turn for guidance is courting disaster.

Things fall apart, the centre cannot hold;
Mere anarchy is loosed upon the world.
The blood-dimmed tide is loosed, and everywhere
The ceremony of innocence is doomed.
The best lack all conviction, while the worst
Are full of passionate intensity.

The truth of Christ's parable leaps out at us with fresh relevance.[1] Men thought that western civilisation could not only stand but actually perpetuate itself, empty, garnished, and swept of every embarrassing religious dogma; but into the resultant vacuum marauding influences in the shape of demoniac ideologies rushed in to take possession. To our bitter cost we soon learned that the last state was much worse than the first.

If we had happened to drop into the reading room of the British Museum about the middle of the last century, we might have seen a bearded man sitting at a table covered with books, furiously taking notes. If we had paid any attention at all, the chances are that we would have dismissed him as a man of no consequence, a continental crank who like thousands of others had found asylum in England. That was indeed how many of his own contemporaries regarded Karl Marx—the man who read and wrote as if the future of the world depended on him alone. There at his accustomed table he hammered out the creed which, within a century, was destined to revolutionise and remake history. This creed, though rooted in religious scepticism, is still amazingly positive. It proclaimed the collapse of a corrupt system, the coming of a new order, and the dawn of a mighty revolution. It asserted that nothing the entrenched bat-

[1]Matt. 12, v. 44; Luke 11, v. 25.

talions of reaction could do would halt its irresistible advance. This creed of Marx, aggressively blasphemous though it was, was nevertheless explosively dynamic. That is why millions were prepared to dedicate themselves to its proclamation and fulfilment.

The Church can never hope to win the war of conflicting ideologies until she possesses a creed not less positive but infinitely more dynamic. The tide of history will not be turned by idealists who pride themselves on how little they believe, nor will the cynical masses be convinced by those who have shorn Christ of His cosmic stature and reduced the religion of the Cross to the level of a well-meaning Rotarian "chumminess". For society as well as for the individual a creed far from being a decorative fringe, is a central basic necessity.

The second fallacy is the one which would divorce creed from conduct. Theology, according to this attitude, is useless and irrelevant. Belief is something secondary and unimportant. Morality is not a by-product of religion, it is absolutely autonomous and its sanctions have nothing whatever to do with the mystical experience of the saints or the traditional dogmas of the Church. Behaviour is what really matters.

Two eminent Victorians are cited to support this theory—John Morley and Thomas Huxley. Both were professedly agnostic, yet no one could point a finger at their morals. Not only were they good living in the conventional sense of that term, they also loved their fellow-men and were prepared to do battle for all good causes. Disciplined in conduct and dedicated to truth these men are held up as having sabotaged the claim that there is any necessary connection between creed and conduct.

But there is one awkward question. Is this kind of morality self-creating and self-sustaining? Will it continue to operate indefinitely under its own momentum?

Does it create enough spiritual capital to provide support for the next generation and the one after? The answer is given by Thomas Huxley's grandson, Aldous in his book, *Ends and Means*. There he confesses that a creedless morality leads in the end to disillusionment and the collapse of inner integrity. An atheist may continue for a time to manifest the fruit of Christian love but at best it is only a temporary phenomenon. After all, as Principal John Baillie writes : " a railway engine does not stop as soon as the driver shuts off the steam, nor does a turnip wither and die as soon as it is pulled out of Mother earth."

Europe within recent memory was shocked by the hideous recrudescence of savagery practised with all the sadistic refinement of modern science. Hitler and his regime liquidated millions of Jews and set up the torture laboratories which went by the name of Buchenwald and Belsen. Civilised men were deeply shocked, but if they had read the signs of the times they should have anticipated such events. Any one who reads *Mein Kampf* can see this barbarous conduct was but the logical consequences of a creed which denied God, and therefore the sanctity of personality.

John Galsworthy sees this very clearly in his novel *Maid in Waiting*. Dinny, discussing religion with her mother, says " Providence is too remote, Mother. It's too remote. I suppose there is an eternal plan but we are like gnats for all the care it has of us." " Don't encourage such feelings, Dinny," replied the mother. " They affect one's character." " I don't see the connection between beliefs and character," answered Dinny. " I am not going to behave any worse because I cease to believe in Providence or in an after-life. If I am decent it's because decency is the decent thing, and not because I'm going to get anything by it." In a way it sounds a reasonable argument but Dinny's mother goes straight to the heart of things by asking, " Yes, but why is decency the decent thing, if there is no God?" The logic is irrefutable. Sanctions only become absolutely binding when they are seen as sanctities. What we are in the long run is determined by what we believe.

The third modern fallacy is that which maintains that Christian belief is a matter of subscribing to certain abstract propositions. A creed is vitally imperative. It serves as an anchor which holds us when we are tossed to and fro at the mercy of changing winds of doctrine and the clash of conflicting opinions. The classical doctrines of the Church must, however, not be despised. They are clear and concise statements of the " faith once delivered unto the saints ", and they were framed and formulated by some of the best minds in history. Nevertheless, important as these doctrines are, they must not be allowed to obscure for us the vital fact that the essence of religion is a direct encounter between two persons—ourselves and the Living God. This is what Martin Buber means when he talks of an " I—Thou relationship ".

We are living in a collectivist age in which most of our human relationships have become depersonalised. It is not surprising then, to find many people thinking and writing of God in impersonal terms. They talk of a Just Cause, an Absolute Principle or a Realm of Values, but such abstractions can never satisfy the hunger of the human soul. The same tendency expresses itself among preachers who wax eloquent about the relevance of Christianity and have little or nothing to say about the claims of Christ.

The God revealed to us in the Bible is intensely personal. He is one to Whom we turn in time of need, " Who forgiveth all Thine iniquities; who healeth all thy diseases."[1] Jesus did not talk about something behind phenomena. He said, "When ye pray, say, 'Our Father'."[2] Paul did not say "I am prepared to sub-

[1]Ps. 103, v. 3.   [2]Luke 11, v. 2.

scribe to a number of abstract propositions defining the nature of Ultimate Reality." He cried from the heart— "For I know Whom I have believed, and am persuaded that He is able to keep that which I have committed unto Him against that day."[1] For the Christian, intellectual assent to a creed is secondary. The essence of the faith is trust in a Personal God Who became incarnate in Jesus Christ.

That is the characteristic difference between Christianity and other religions. Confucianism is a collection of ethical maxims. Mohammedanism is the religion of a book rigidly interpreted and absolutely binding on its devotees. Christianity is the religion, not of a book but of a Person. Jesus commissioned His Apostles and established His Church before there were any written records of His earthly ministry. Christians in the last resort are asked to give their allegiance—not to any dogma or abstract article of belief, but to the Living Lord, the Risen Christ, Who still speaks and communes with His believing people.

[1] II Timothy 1, v. 12.

CHAPTER 7

DOCTRINE OF MAN

WHAT IS man? The answer that he is a puzzling contradiction would command a large measure of agreement. No doubt he is, as the Psalmist asserts, a little lower than the angels, but he is also a devil incarnate who in a Gestapo or Ogpu uniform takes sadistic delight in torturing and destroying his fellow humans.

The profoundest minds have always been conscious of this baffling dichotomy. Shakespeare reflects—" What a piece of work is a man, how noble in reason, how infinite in faculty, and in form how moving, how express and admirable, in action how like an angel, in apprehension how like a god !" But elsewhere he contemptuously talks of man :

> Drest in a little brief authority;
> Most ignorant of what he is most assured.
> His glassy essence, like an angry ape,
> Plays such fantastic tricks before high heaven
> As make the angels weep.

Pascal, too, was aware of this duality. He writes : " What a chimera is man then ! What a novelty, what a monster, what a chaos, what a subject of contradiction, what a prodigy ! Judge of all things, imbecile earthworm, depository of the truth, sewer of uncertainty and error, glory and refuse of the universe."

And Paul expresses the enigma with characteristic force. " I find then a law, that, when I would do good, evil is present with me. For I delight in the law of God

52

after the inward man. But I see another law in my members, warring against the law of my mind, and bringing me into captivity to the law of sin which is in my members."[1]

It is no longer possible to pretend that a contradiction does not exist. Every new invention like the aeroplane and discovery like the splitting of the atom brings home to us with a sort of shuddering impact the realisation that there is something radically wrong with human nature. Modern man is prepared to admit this but he ascribes the contradiction to a combination of causes which he believes time can remedy.

One such cause he claims is the evolutionary lag. This theory rests on the assumption that what the theologians call sin is merely a survival of our animal heritage. It is the resultant of physical passions and vital impulses but once man acquires a civilised veneer, the downward drag of heredity will gradually disappear.

The fallacy at the heart of this view is belief that sin is essentially animal, not human. Dostoievsky, in his novel *The Brothers Karamazov* tears this myth to tatters. He makes one of his characters say : "A Bulgarian I met lately in Moscow told me of the crime committed by Turks and Caucasians in Bulgaria through fear of a general rising of the Slavs—They burn villages, outrage women and children; they nail prisoners by the ear to the fences, leave them there till the morning, and in the morning they hang them—all sorts of things you can't imagine. People talk sometimes of bestial cruelty, but that is a grave injustice and insult to the beasts. A beast can never be as cruel as a man, as artistically cruel. The tiger only tears and gnaws —that is all he can do, but he would never think of nailing people by the ear even were he able to do it." The logic of that is unanswerable—sin by its very nature is distinctively human.

[1]Romans 7, v. 21 ff.

Another alleged cause of the hiatus between dream and reality is social injustice. Here we confront a strange paradox. The contemporary conscience on social questions is sharp and insistent and imperious, whereas in the realm of private morality it is almost atrophied. For a large section of mankind to-day, sin and social inequality are synonymous.

The secular prophets confidently predicted that once justice was established all temptation towards acquisitiveness and self-aggrandisement would automatically disappear. The truth proved to be very different. The Czars went out and the Commissars came in. A Marie Antoinette is invariably followed by a Napoleon. Studdert Kennedy once made the shrewd observation that when a country changes its government, it only pushes one set of sinners out and puts another set of sinners in. The most passionate idealists are never completely free from egocentricity and partisan bias. Berdyaev, the modern philosopher, once an ardent Communist who attached tremendous importance to the part legislation could play in any community, was under no illusion when he said " There is something demonic in human nature ". We would be much nearer the mark were we to claim that the contradiction standing at the heart of society is of the very essence of sin, and not the product of an abstraction like social injustice.

Still again there are many who maintain that the spanner in the works is inadequate education. This view is as old as Plato but it is widely held in the twentieth century. Bertrand Russell of Britain and John Dewey of America are among its most eloquent apostles. J. B. S. Haldane sees no limit to its possibilities. He actually argues that, under its influence, " man will be able to think like Newton, to write like Racine, to paint like the Van Eycks, to compose like Bach. They will be incapable of hatred as St. Francis."

He overlooked the corruption of man's heart which

can employ education as an instrument of its own selfish designs, as a decoration for social prestige, or as a means for professional advantage. Both Nazis and Communists used it to buttress their own particular ideologies, while in liberal countries there is danger of education degenerating into a formula of adjustment to meet the increasing demands of technology.

Anyhow, the educated man is not necessarily a good man. Sin can take on a high polish and speak with impeccable logic in the suavest of accents. It was not untutored savages but the products of western civilisation who were responsible for the last two wars. The mad holocaust that destroyed millions of precious lives and did untold moral and psychological harm took place on the most educated of all continents. And to-day we are not afraid of primitive people, but of men who possess the technical know-how to threaten the existence of the human race. While the Christian welcomes the civilising and liberating influence of education in society, he nevertheless holds that it does not provide the answer. The curse of Adam, the dilemma of personality, the central contradiction of human nature, demand something more radical.

The ancient Greeks had a myth which tells how the Titans, a race of giants, plotted an assault on heaven. Armed with rocks and firebrands they hurled themselves against the gods and nearly won the battle. But the Olympians stood fast. The arrows of Heracles and the thunderbolts of Zeus proved decisive, and the Titans were in the end destroyed.

According to Karl Barth, the real sin of the twentieth century is " Titanism." Modern man, he claims, is not a sheep which has temporarily strayed from the paths of righteousness; not a muddle-headed but well-meaning creature who can be lured back to the fold by what the misguided call " the reasonableness of Christianity ". That, says Barth, is sentimental twaddle, and here I feel we must applaud his good sense. The men who liquidated millions of Jews and experimented on women and children with deadly germs in the interests of scientific medicine, were not sheep bleating in momentary perplexity, but Titans who declared war on God, and plotted an assault on heaven. Sin, whatever name we give it, is enmity against God. It is the putting of the Ego on the throne of the Universe, and the expelling of God from the place which is His by right.

At this point we must be careful not to come to too easy terms with the doctrine of total depravity. That original sin is a stubborn and ineradicable fact any one with a knowledge of history is bound to admit. It is not just the individual that is wrong. He is born into a world of disorder that infects him from the first, shaping his thoughts and conditioning most of his reflexes. The doctrine of original sin is not a strain on a reasonable man's credulity. But that of total depravity is different. Its sponsors would have us believe that human nature has no redeeming qualities, that it is an abode of darkness out of which not even the faintest gleam of light or goodness ever shines. Now while we repudiate utopianism in any shape or form and reject all facile explanation of the human dilemma, we must on no account succumb to a thorough-going pessimism regarding man himself. John Baillie is surely right in reminding us that a totally corrupt being would be as incapable of sin as would a totally illogical being of fallacious argument. But there is a sense in which the doctrine of total depravity is right. It is not part but the totality of man's being that is affected by sin. His will and intellect and emotions are infected by this disease and even the purest of the human graces can become the instrument of an evil which permeates the whole of our morbid existence.

That is one side of the truth about men, but there is another side which must be stressed in an age which tempts us to lose faith in human possibilities. Man can descend to abysmal depths of cruelty, sadism and sinister conduct but like the prodigal in the far country he is not inevitably lost. He is still capable of self-criticism and even of saying : " I will arise and go to my Father ".[1] No system of theology that ignores this paradoxical fact has anything of importance to contribute to our generation. There is an indissoluble kinship between God and man. It is a contradiction in terms to talk of " godless man " for his very humanity implies that he stands in a unique relationship with the divine. This is more than metaphor; it is a fact rooted in the history of the human race and capable of standing up to the fiercest scrutiny.

That man has always possessed an ineradicable sense of the divine rests on evidence which in its cumulative effect is simply overwhelming. The records and relics of the past, the researches of anthropologists into the beliefs and customs of primitive people, all testify to the universality of this urge. Julian Huxley, no orthodox believer, begs science to admit " the psychology of religion as an ultimate fact." Nor has the ascendancy of science and the advance of knowledge done anything to weaken this immemorial sense of kinship. Civilisations may crumble into dust, sacrosanct philosophies hallowed by time may lose their potency, the face of society may undergo the most radical change, but man still continues to cry : " Oh, that I knew where I might find him !"[2] It is thought-provoking that in America, where applied science has a stronger hold over people's daily living than anywhere else in the world, church attendance is higher to-day than it was at the time of the Pilgrim Fathers.

According to the New Testament, man is an ambivalent creature. The serpent has him by the head, but the angel has him by the hand. He may live a riotously

[1] Luke 15, v. 18.   [2] Job 23, v. 3.

undisciplined life, squandering his gifts and prostituting his talents, but he is not beyond redemption. He is still capable of crying out of the depths of a God-tormented soul " I will arise and go to my Father!"

The message of the Incarnation is two-fold. Jesus Christ, it declares, is the Revelation of the true nature of God, and also the revelation of the true nature of man. Human nature has been corrupted by sin. It has become defaced and tarnished, but it can be redeemed. There is no condoning of evil in the Gospels, not any blurring of moral distinctions, but in the parables one looks in vain for the belief that everything in man is foul and beastly and depraved. In a world where injustice seems so strong and triumphant, we may find it hard to accept the New Testament conception of God, but in a world where human folly is contemplating mass suicide, we may find it even harder to accept the New Testament conception of man. John lived in desperately wicked days, but he writes " Now are we the sons of God, and it doth not yet appear what we shall be."[1] Paul, who in the first chapter of his epistle to the Romans, stresses the grim and demonic reality of sin, nevertheless writes : " Till we all come in the unity of the faith, and of the knowledge of the Son of God, unto a perfect man, unto the measure of the stature of the fulness of Christ."[2] The human situation in these days lights up one central and everlasting truth—man's moral impotence and Christ's triumphant adequacy.

[1] I John 3, v. 2.   [2] Ephesians 4, v. 13.

CHAPTER 8

AGONY OF FAITH

JOHN HENRY NEWMAN somewhere claims that he cannot remember ever having doubted the existence of God. He belonged to the fortunate few to whom faith in a Supreme Being is as self-evident as the proposition that two multiplied by two make four.

At the other end of the scale, Swinburne, parading an aggressive atheism, could write :

Thou art smitten, Thou God, Thou art smitten;
Thy death is upon Thee, O Lord,
And the live songs of earth as Thou diest
Resound through the wind of her wings—
Glory to man in the highest, for man is the master
*   of things.*

Most of us find ourselves in a position somewhere between the two. We lack the sublime assurance of the one and the swaggering self-confidence of the other. We are divided personalities, victims of tensions and conflicts which pull us in different directions. Our faith is never constant; it is a pendulum at the mercy of changing circumstances—the state of our health, the pressures of life, and the psychological mood of the moment.

The great geniuses, with their penetrating insight into human nature, have always been aware of this inner conflict. Shakespeare poses it in Hamlet, Goethe in Faust, Dostoievsky in Ivan Karamazov. With Job they would all agree that faith, far from being easy, is born of anguish and travail of soul.

This is the avowed confession of some of the most eminent Christian thinkers of our day. William Temple was so tormented with doubts that he waited for years and engaged in a heart-searching correspondence with the Archbishop of Canterbury before he eventually felt he could, with a clear conscience, proceed to ordination. Principal David Cairns of Aberdeen passed through a somewhat similar experience. This is how he describes it in his autobiography : " I have a vivid snapshot of myself standing beneath a flaring gas jet in my bedroom at Lonsdale Terrace, absolutely dismayed. What reason had I for believing in God, or Christ, or immortality? I had, I thought, none. But if there was no God, there was only a horror of great darkness, a wide grey lampless, deep, unpeopled world. I entered here a long dark tunnel of my life from which I only gradually emerged." John Baillie, in an excellent portrait of his late brother Donald, admits that the man whom many regarded as a fine combination of saint and scholar, was haunted by doubt even to the end. He would say : " When the darkness is on me I walk down the street and see people walking aimlessly about, and shops, and cars and a few dogs, and it all seems to me nothing and to matter not at all."

The classic expression of this tension between faith and doubt is found in the New Testament. The father of the epileptic boy was prepared to do anything to restore his son to health. When Jesus told him recovery demanded a measure of faith on his part, he blurted out the honest answer : " Lord, I believe; help Thou mine unbelief."[1] This agonising cry wrung from the depth of a tormented soul is imperishable because it speaks to man's condition in every passing age.

All men in their best moments want to believe, but the

[1]Mark 9, v. 24.

obstacles in the way of faith are formidable and difficult to surmount. We tend to become mesmerised by
them to the exclusion of all else.

Which of us has not looked up on a starry evening
to the infinite number of universes that crowd space,
and has not felt that these stellar immensities reduce our
individual lives to the utmost insignificance? What is
this tiny infinitesimal earth, smaller in comparison than
a speck of dust, and who are we to suppose ourselves
the special objects of Providential care?

Or who among us has not been conscious of the
presence of evil—endemic in the very constitution of
the world, and not been made aware of it as a deliberate
diabolical force that mocks our holiest dreams, and
sabotages our best laid schemes? It is stronger than
human sin, asserts Paul. " For we wrestle not against
flesh and blood but against principalities, against powers,
against the rulers of the darkness of this world, against
spiritual wickedness in high places."[1] The late C. E. M.
Joad sums up the conundrum succinctly : " If God is
all powerful and permits evil, He is not good. If He
is good and permits evil, He is not all-powerful."

There is, too, the enigma of suffering. If God is in
control, why does He allow it? To say its purpose is
to create character is not a convincing argument. What
parent would deliberately inoculate his child with a
deadly germ in order to strengthen his moral fibre?
In Albert Camus's novel, *The Plague,* there is a gripping
scene where a doctor, a priest, and a high-minded agnostic stand round the bed of a little boy dying of the
bubonic plague. The frail little body is writhing in
agony. The small pitiful face has become rigid as a
mask of greyish clay. The priest, hiding his face in his
hands, prays " God, spare the child ". But he dies in
convulsions. Later, sitting under the swaying branches
of the trees in the hospital garden, the priest breaks

[1] Ephesians 6, v. 12.

the heavy silence : " That sort of thing is revolting,
because it passes human understanding, but perhaps we
should try to love what we cannot understand." The
doctor, normally an even-tempered man, turned on him
like a tiger and said : " No, Father ! I have a very
different idea of love and until my dying day I refuse
to believe in a God Who lets a child die like that."

We have all at some time or another experienced the
assault of doubt. Like Wordsworth, we too have been
conscious of

> . . . *the burthen of the mystery*
> . . . *the heavy and the weary weight*
> *Of all this unintelligible world.*

But all this is only one side of the tension of faith.
There is another which is equally compelling. It is
true that we stand dumb before the dark tremendous
facts which shake our souls, but we are also aware of
psychological and moral compulsions which drive us
willy-nilly in the direction of God. We have felt the
Everlasting Yea rising up within us and choking back
the Everlasting Nay. It is because we have wrestled
with doubt in the dark places of life that we understand
the transparently honest cry " Lord, I believe; help
Thou mine unbelief."[1]

However self-sufficient a man may imagine himself
to be, in his more serious moments he secretly longs for
spiritual reinforcement. Need speaks to different men
in different ways. To one man it comes through a
crushing consciousness of guilt. He has betrayed his
ideals, disobeyed his conscience, and in his heart he
knows the facile formulae and glib rationalisations of
worldly wisdom only mock his desperate malaise. The
only remedy lies in forgiveness, and forgiveness cannot be mediated by an abstract First Cause or a remote

[1]Mark. 9, v. 24.

Absolute Principle, but by a Personal God. "For He knoweth our frame; He remembereth that we are dust."[1]

To another, need comes through a sharp sense of inner inadequacy. Like the father of the epileptic boy in the Gospels, he suddenly realises he lacks all power to heal himself or anyone else. He has his ideal of a strong masterful character but he finds himself crying with Tennyson:

> *Ah, for a man to arise in me*
> *That the man I am, may cease to be.*

And beneath all his outward scepticism he knows religion is a source of limitless spiritual power. Down the passing centuries it has made men adequate for every test and crisis of life, and changed human weakness into strength. So Isaiah, living in a turbulent era cried, "They that wait upon the Lord shall renew their strength; they shall mount up with wings as eagles; they shall run, and not be weary; and they shall walk, and not faint."[2] So, St. Paul, facing execution, found himself adequate, "strengthened with might by His Spirit in the inner man."[3]

Another strong compulsion is that of truth. Any system of thought, political, economic or theological, that opposes truth is under sentence of death.

The truth may be thwarted and perverted by evil men. For whole generations, even centuries, it may be driven underground, but in the end it is always irresistible. Men like Copernicus, Galileo, Newton and Wilberforce, were maligned and persecuted by their contemporaries, but the truth they proclaimed won the day and history has vindicated them to the full.

And why is Jesus so much at home in the age of the atom as He was in rural Palestine? The answer surely is because He is the truth and the truth is indestructible.

[1]Ps. 103, v. 14. [2]Isaiah 40, v. 31. [3]Ephesians 3, v. 16.

Men went to desperate lengths to destroy Him. They crucified Him and buried Him in a strongly guarded tomb, but this could not silence Him. That is the mystery and the power of truth. Men may crucify it and bury it, and roll the heavy stone of a moribund tradition on top of it, but it always rises again. Therein lies the inescapable challenge of the Christian religion. In Jesus Christ we meet not a spiritual phenomenon struck off by the chance collision of physical forces, but Truth Incarnate.

And to the compulsions of need and truth I myself would add that of choice. One of the tensest moments of the whole of the Second World War was on Sunday night, the 4th of June, 1944, the eve of the cross-channel invasion. With a sky badly overcast, poor visibility and a heavy swell out at sea, experts predicted a deterioration of the weather. Postpone or proceed—this was the momentous question. Postponement meant large scale disorganisation, loss of security, and a shattering of morale keyed up to fighting pitch. On the other hand, invasion in adverse conditions might mean irretrievable failure, and indiscriminate slaughter on strongly defended enemy beaches. The final decision was left till 4.15 a.m. on Monday morning. The latest weather reports were read. The meteorological experts gave their opinion, and all eyes turned to General Eisenhower sitting at the end of the table in the Operation Room. For nearly a minute no one spoke. The silence was electric, charged as it were with destiny. The outcome of the war, the future of Europe, the fate of millions of men depended on the decision of one man suddenly made lonely by this crushing load of responsibility. At length it came clear and colloquial, but positive—" O.K. We'll go."

Life scorns neutrality of any shade or colour. For this very reason agnosticism is the most pathetic of all possible attitudes. We may remain uncommitted regarding many questions. We may not be able to decide whether we prefer the episcopalian or the presbyterian system of Church government, the theologies of Barth or of Brunner. Fundamentally that is not very important. But life is different. Like a swift moving stream it flows on irresistibly, carrying us along on its turbulent surface, and whether we are aware of it or not, we are deciding either for a paralysing scepticism or a dynamic faith.

Spiritually, morally, psychologically, commitment is imperative. In his book *The Principles of Psychology,* William James writes : " We are spinning our own fates, good or evil, and never to be undone. The drunken Rip Van Winkle in Jefferson's play excuses himself for every fresh dereliction by saying " I won't count this time." Well, he may not count it and a kind Heaven may not count it, but it is being counted none the less. Down among his nerve cells and fibres, the molecules are counting it, registering it and storing it up to be used against him when the next temptation comes." Life itself is commitment. Jesus had this in mind when He said " He that is not with Me is against Me."[1] And the question we have to answer is whether we are to maintain a spurious neutrality or else cry :

Whoso hath felt the Spirit of the Highest
Cannot confound or doubt Him, or deny.
Yea with one voice, O World, though thou deniest,
Stand then on that side, for on this am I.

[1]*Matt.* 12, v. 30; Luke 11, v. 23.

CHAPTER 9

PRIORITY OF GOD

SIGNIFICANTLY enough the Bible wastes no time on discussing atheism, but it is preoccupied almost to the point of obsession with idolatry. The outstanding idols of the Old Testament are Ashera, goddess of the high places; Baal, the god of fertility, and Moloch, god of sacrifice, into whose fiery furnace countless humans were thrown.

The Greeks also had their temples dedicated to the gods—Minerva, goddess of wisdom; Bacchus, god of wine; Apollo, god of physical beauty; Venus, goddess of love. The Romans, too, had their pantheon where Mars, god of war and Lares and Penates, the gods of hearth and home were accorded divine honours.

Those of us who consider ourselves rigid monotheists, look with pity on primitive peoples who crowded heaven and earth with a grotesque assortment of deities. We no longer gather round sacred trees, assemble in dark haunted groves, or prostrate ourselves before gem-encrusted statues of peevish divinities. These are superstitions which belong to the past. We are now emancipated.

But are we as emancipated as we think we are? We tend to forget that in remote times gods were only names for clamorous desires, passionate devotions, fundamental loyalties. We miss the point because we think of idols in terms of images and statues and forget that what really mattered was the inner aim and objective behind the physical objects.

The passions which once found expression in multiple gods and carved idols are by no means out of date. We take it for granted that idolatry is obsolete, but it is only obsolete in its outer forms. We are apt to overlook the fact that the ancient Semites, Greeks and Romans in erecting idols were only externalising their deep psychological urges. These are the same yesterday, to-day and for ever; only their expressions now are more subtle and they are camouflaged under different names.

Take the State for example. In an incredibly short space of time, it has become transformed from an institution, sensitive to criticism, into a cast-iron totalitarian system that rides rough-shod over men's most sacred beliefs. Shortly before the First World War, a German officer knocked into the gutter a lame cobbler who did not make way for him in the little town of Zabern. The incident was reported throughout the world, and so incensed were people by this expression of military ruthlessness, that the German Government censured the whole Army for the conduct of one of its members. That was in 1913. By 1936 there were extermination camps all over Germany and only a handful of people protested.

The entire English speaking world was profoundly shocked by what came to be known as McCarthyism. McCarthy is dead, it is true, but there are many discerning Americans who know that though his body, like John Brown's, is mouldering in the grave, his soul goes marching on. McCarthy is only one symptom of a deep-seated malignant disease which is eating away the body of democracy itself. Britain has by no means escaped. The knowledge that our "free" universities are subject to a measure of secret service surveillance is, to say the least of it, disturbing. But, it may be argued that the unscruplous tactics of a ruthless enemy justifies such security measures. Admittedly vigilance is imperative, but it is a sorry look-out for any freedom-loving country when it is compelled to adopt the clandestine espionage methods of totalitarian governments. The

State has become an idol, and our only real protection
against it is an alert and intelligent Christian conscience.

Technology comes next in the pantheon of modern
gods. Like the State, it is fundamentally a good thing,
but in the hands of evil men it can become a Franken-
stein. Eminent scientists and theologians are constantly
asserting that the gulf between science and religion is
narrower than it has ever been. Theoretically speaking, that is so, but on a practical level there is no doubt
as to which has the pre-eminence. The new god, Technology, threatens to become omnipotent. When a
government is faced with a crisis, and launches a new
drive, it is invariably for technologists, not for theologians, and, in a way, the government is right. If
Britain is to retain her position in the world, she must
have scientists and more scientists, but this need is one
more reminder that among modern idols, Technology
stands supreme.

The competitive race in producing bigger and better
hydrogen bombs is an even grimmer reminder that technology, unless it is controlled by wise men, may in the
end lead to the annihilation of the race. The real danger of the hydrogen bomb lies in the dreadful possibility that it may set up a chain reaction not in space but
in the human mind. A succession of explosions may
remove the last of our humanitarian inhibitions. Scientists themselves admit that they have created a Franken-
stein which may turn in the end to destroy them and
all the achievements of man unless it is banned while
there is yet time. This is one dangerous modern idol
that must be destroyed before it destroys us.

The third god worshipped in our modern pantheon is
Mammon. Mammon in the Bible stands for money-
making, the spirit of unbridled acquisitiveness and
worldly ambition. This ancient god claims to-day more
disciples and devotees than ever before. Mammonism
(along with the twin god Mechanism) has been and

still is one of the chief moulders of character. Money has become the symbol of power, and in our time, power is the chief end of man. Dickens in *Hard Times* in his classic portrait of Bounderby, paints the typical worshipper of Mammon in harsh, unrelieved colours. Bounderby believed in work and production and profit-making as ends in themselves. For him, activity was not rhythmically counter-balanced by contemplation. He had only one definite aim in life—to make more and more money. Sinclair Lewis's portrait of Babbit, slave of slick gadgets and mechanised comfort, is the American twentieth century equivalent. Bounderby and Babbit have this in common—they are disciples of Mammon. They both break the First Commandment in that at the end of a busy week they have no energy left to cultivate any higher interests. The one is the incarnation of utilitarianism naked and unrelieved; the other of a utilitarianism debased and de-energised, but both the end result of Mammon worship. The appeal of gambling to millions and the astronomical sums of money that exchange hands in the pools, for example, provide further tragic evidence of the universal sway of Mammon.

Finally, there is the good of self. This is the most dangerous and most powerful of all the idols because it is the most subtle and it is more devouring than Moloch ever was. The ancient Greeks illustrate the morbid preoccupation with self in their legend of the youth Narcissus who fell in love with his own image in a fountain. We are all to some extent guilty of Narcissism. Some people gaze at their own reflection in the fountain of their achievements. They are inordinately proud of the fact that as a result of industry and perseverance they have attained their present success. Others gaze at their own reflection in the fountain of their social status. With pagans this ambition is understandable; but the length to which some Christians

will go to cultivate the "right people" and to belong
to the right set, borders on the blasphemous. Others
still gaze at their own reflection in the fountain of
the family. If the children are blessed with good looks,
they have inherited them; if they are clever it is again
a matter of heredity; if they succeed in life the parents
bask in reflected glory. The paradox is that the family,
the most sacred of all human institutions, can become
a vehicle of arrogance and an extension of the naked
ego. No man can call himself free till he has dethroned
and driven out this idol of self.

Perhaps we are now beginning to understand why
Christianity is so pathetically ineffective in the modern
world. Christians have forgotten, first of all, the commandment "Thou shalt have no other gods before
me."[1] In actual practice they unwittingly are polythe-
ists worshipping multiple idols. These are the gods that
call forth their deepest loyalties and their sacrificial
devotion. God the Father of our Lord Jesus Christ has
become for many a marginal reference, a decorative
embellishment; an expendable luxury, not the axis
round which our world revolves.

The Bible denounces idolatry because idols destroy
the cohesion of society and disintegrate the fabric of
personality. The First Commandment is as relevant to-
day as it was when the Great Lawgiver led the children
of Israel across the desert to the borders of the Pro-
mised Land. Men must give their loyalty to church,
state and family, but their deepest devotion must be
given to God. God comes first.

He comes first because He covers the whole of life.
"In His Hand", said the Psalmist, "are the deep
places of the earth."[2] He is all-embracing. There is
no aspect of reality with which He is not concerned.
He is the Sovereign Lord of the Universe, towering

[1]Exodus 20, v. 3.   [2]Ps. 95, v. 4.

above our human institutions, transcending man's highest hopes and aspirations.

He comes first because He is ultimately reliable. He never lets us down. Our human idols are deceptive and illusory. They are the shadow and not the substance. Even the staunchest of friends can fail us at times, but "with God ' is no variableness, neither shadow of turning.' "[1] ... He is " the same yesterday, and to-day, and for ever."[2]

He comes first because He can save to the uttermost. Idols divide and in the end turn us into schizophrenics. God, on the other hand, when He becomes the focus of our interests and our energies, integrates personality. Modern man may not, like the Philippian gaoler in the throes of an earthquake, ask " Sirs, what must I do to be saved?"[3] but when he goes to the consulting room of the psychiatrist, he is unconsciously asking the same question. The psychiatrist does not have the answer. It was given us long ago in the First Commandment: " I am the Lord thy God. . . . Thou shalt have no other gods before me."

[1]James 1, v. 17.   [2]Heb. 13, v. 8.   [3]Acts 16, v. 30.

CHAPTER 10

GREATNESS OF GOD

SOCRATES, the wisest man of antiquity, whom one of the early Church fathers called a Christian before Christ, was tried and condemned to death for atheism. But his last words to the jury that passed sentence were these: "No evil can happen to a good man either in life or after death. His fortunes are not neglected by God." Socrates, as we know now, was not an unbeliever; he had only rebelled against the superstitious crudities of contemporary religion.

The early Christians were also accused of atheism. When Polycarp, Bishop of Smyrna, was led out to martyrdom about the year A.D. 150, his executioners tried to make him cry "Away with the atheists!"—meaning by that his fellow believers. Again we know that they were regarded as atheists because their beliefs conflicted with the popular conception of pagan gods.

And to-day many self-styled atheists are only inwardly rebelling against grotesque caricatures of the deity which cannot stand up to critical scrutiny. Like Socrates in ancient Athens, they have turned their backs on the grosser forms of popular belief, but unlike him they have not attained to a living, personal faith.

It is possible for intelligent men to spend a good deal of their time tilting against an imaginary god, and to convince themselves in the process that they cannot be orthodox Christians. This emerges in the intensely interesting correspondence between the late Principal David Cairns of Aberdeen and the distinguished Professor of English Literature, Sir Herbert Grierson. The latter clearly shows that he had rebelled against some of the traditional formulations of orthodoxy. Cairns is most sympathetic and more than gracious in his replies, but in one of his letters he claims that Sir Herbert is revolting against crude and false caricatures of the one and only God. He writes : " Therefore, I close . . . with a clear definition of what I mean when I say ' God.' I don't mean God as conceived by half-barbaric Spaniards chanting in Toledo Cathedral or even by Scholastic Puritans. I mean the God and Father of our Lord Jesus Christ, and our God and Father in Him. Explicated, I find that means, that I think of Him :

(a) as One Who is in Supreme control (Sovereign)
(b) as One Who is always incomparably better than the very best we can think of Him, and finally
(c) that He is not simply static goodness, but that He is gracious."

Whether we like it or not we are living in an age of revolution when many of our cherished notions have been overthrown. Miracles of invention and technical mastery happen with such bewildering rapidity that we are in danger of losing our capacity for surprise, and becoming blasé. Now, more than ever before, we need to enlarge our conception of the deity.

The God we profess must be big enough intellectually. Few of us have either the mental equipment or the necessary training to examine or explore the universe around us, but we are indebted to scientists like Sir Arthur Eddington, Sir James Jeans and Fred Hoyle for their brilliant gifts of popular exposition. They somehow or other manage to break down for us abstract mathematical formulae and bring home to us in the most vivid manner the magnitude and mystery of the universe.

What they reveal gives a severe jolt to the conventional mind. It becomes clear that we should talk not of one but of an infinite number of universes. The imagination staggers before the innumerable multitude of planets, the unthinkable distances measured only in light years. According to Hoyle, some of the receding galaxies are travelling away from us at a rate of over two hundred million miles an hour. In the midst of it all there is the tiny infinitesimal earth, smaller in comparison than one grain of sand on all the sea-shores of the world.

These startling revelations on the part of modern physics and astronomy have induced in Christians a spirit of humility which they sadly lacked when a few centuries ago Copernicus and Galileo announced their far-reaching discoveries. In the past the Church was guilty of defending to the death positions which were intellectually indefensible, and of proclaiming a God too limited to cope with discoveries full of revolutionary implications for mankind.

The Christian must be a man who cultivates within himself a blend of deep humility and absolute confidence. On the one hand, he must welcome all new truths whether they come from the examination of microscopic matter or the exploration of outer space. On the other hand he must be fortified with the unshakable conviction that no new discovery, however momentous, will ever separate him from the love of God.

The God revealed in the Bible can never be superseded because He is the Maker of heaven and earth. The prophet Isaiah would not have been disturbed by the disclosures of our long-range telescopes. Did he not reassure us of the absolute greatness of God when he wrote " Lift up your eyes on high, and behold who hath created these things, that bringeth out their host by number : He calleth them all by names by the greatness of his might, for that He is strong in power; not one faileth."[1] God is greater than all our human formulae and discoveries, so we can face the future and all it holds in a spirit of absolute confidence.

[1]Isaiah 40, v. 26.

Our little systems have their day,
They have their day and cease to be.
They are but broken lights of Thee
And Thou, O Lord, art more than they.

Again, the God we profess must be big enough ethi-
cally. This does not mean that God has changed. He
is, in the language of Scripture, without "variableness,
neither shadow of turning",[1] or in the words of the
Shorter Catechism, He is "infinite, eternal and un-
changeable in His Being, Wisdom, Power, Holiness, Justice, Goodness and Truth." But what has changed is
our conception of God from the human side.

At one stage the ancient Hebrews associated the
presence of their God with Mount Sinai. Then they
occupied Palestine, and came to conceive Him of as a
national Deity with his dwelling place on Mount Zion
in Jerusalem. It was not till much later that the
Psalmist sang :

If I ascend up into Heaven, Thou art there.
If I make my bed in hell, behold, Thou art there.
If I take the wings of the morning,
And dwell in the uttermost parts of the sea;
Even there shall Thy hand lead me,
And Thy right hand shall hold me.[2]

This splendid universalism developing through the
Old Testament culminates in the New, where God
is revealed as the Father of all the children of men.

Hand in hand with this universalism of religion goes
a deepening and an extending of its ethical implications.
Indeed the worth of any religion can be fairly adequately
assessed by the depth and range of its ethical impera-
tives.

Christians who believe in God the Father Almighty

[1]James i, v. 17.   [2]Ps. 139, v. 7 l.l.

cannot rest happy with a world rigidly divided into an Eastern and Western bloc, nor can they delude themselves into thinking that a precarious policy of co-existence is the best we can hope for in this world. They must subject not only Communism but also Capitalism to the fiercest scrutiny and judge them both in the light of the revelation of Christ. The Christian ethic must on no account be equated with the Western way of life. God is the Creator and Redeemer of all men, and Christ died for the Russians and the Japanese as well as for the British and Americans.

Nor can Christians be content with a mere private morality. In the past, too many so-called Christians endorsed Lord Melbourne's fixed idea that religion was a private concern and should not be mixed up with politics or social issues. For long the State was supposed to exist for the purpose of protecting the nation from attack from without and the citizens from disturbance from within. Now the State has its pre-natal clinics, its dental and medical inspection of schools, its welfare systems for all ages from the cradle to the grave.

And if the State surrounds the individual with such security, how can we who profess Christ, show less care? As Canon Raven says : "The Church has no business to be a little 'Pleasant Sunday Afternoon' gathering of people living in an ivory tower. It has no business to separate itself from the sins and sufferings, the pain and wants of the world. Jesus lived out His Ministry going about 'doing good', healing all manner of sickness, and ministering to the poor. If we regard ourselves as a privileged community, engaged primarily in religious activities on Sunday, we are denying the belief in the Word made flesh."

The God we profess must be big enough ecclesiastically. At no point does the stature of God suffer more than at the point where our sectarian differences become visible to a critical world. What disillusions the thoughtful outsider is not denominational divisions,—he is prepared to make allowances for that,—but their tendency at times towards exclusiveness and arrogance. He feels that no particular denomination has a monopoly of the grace of God : none can justifiably claim it and it alone possesses the one recipe that can produce Christian character.

To be sure, the Ecumenical movement is moving in the right direction. Its impact was felt even before 1914 and ever since the last War it has gathered momentum. This increasing desire to heal the broken Body of the Church is no accident, it is the work of the Holy Spirit shaming us out of our parochial mentality and pointing us to the oneness which inheres in Christ. It may not be able to boast of great dramatic gains, but nevertheless its achievements have been substantial and the seed now planted promises to bear fruit in future. But it will be baulked and thwarted all along the line unless the organised churches are smitten by a vision of God, high and lifted up, transcending all local and historical limitations.

Canon Raven in the second volume of his Gifford Lectures, claims that this rigid exclusiveness and arrogance is a misunderstanding of the doctrine of the Holy Spirit. " In no other aspect has there been so obvious and continuing a perversion; the gift of the Spirit, from being an abiding life ' in Christ ' with God and the brethren, becomes in popular esteem first a talisman admitting to membership of the Church here and of heaven hereafter, and then a synonym for the privileges which the hierarchy is permitted to bestow, and finally a magical influence conveyed by the appropriate manual contact. If this be thought an exaggeration let the critic of it consider in the light of an honest valuation of human worth the argumentations of ecclesiastics about the fate of the unbaptised, the validity of sacraments and the doctrine of apostolic succession. For it is surely impossible to believe that anyone accustomed to weighing evidence can assert that all members of the Society of Friends are damned or even are outside the Church; that Presbyterian sacraments are not effective symbols and instruments of Christ's presence; and that the religious quality and destiny of Christians are conditional upon the precise method by which the officers of the denomination to which they belong are chosen and consecrated. Yet all these contentions are logically inherent in Catholic orthodoxy."

Our supreme need is a more adequate vision of the Christ Who was the revelation of God the Father Almighty. The impression He made on His own contemporaries was one of bigness. He burst the bounds of their legalism, their provincialism, their nationalism, their cast-iron dogmatism. That is why His enemies crucified Him, and His disciples called Him Divine. This Christ still towers above our world. He impresses even sceptics with His universal range and sweep. No Church which makes petty exclusive claims can worthily or adequately represent the Christ Who ate with publicans and sinners, and Who died on Calvary, not for a select ecclesiastical coterie but for all mankind.

CHAPTER II

FATHERHOOD OF GOD

MEN STILL argue about the existence of God. They even write books on the subject. Some do so in an attempt to demolish the traditionally accepted dogmas; others, taking the opposite side maintain that the existence of God can be proved by the very arguments which their opponents reject. But on the level of mere human enquiry the great enigma remains as insoluble as ever. We have not advanced much further than Job who cried in anguish : " Oh that I knew where I might find Him !"[1] Omar Khayyam's experience strikes a sympathetic chord in every mind that has wrestled with this age-old mystery :

> *Myself when young did eagerly frequent*
> *Doctor and saint, and heard great argument*
> *About it and about, but ever more*
> *Came out by the same door as in I went.*

Now it is both significant and challenging that Jesus never once argued about the existence of God. We search the Gospels in vain for any of the traditional proofs. *Is God Evident?*—the title of a book on natural theology by Gerald Heard, is a question absolutely alien to the thinking of the New Testament.

There was no need to argue. Jesus was a Jew of the first century, and his contemporaries took the existence of God for granted. Monotheism, the belief in One God Who recognised no rival, was deeply ingrained in

[1]Job 23, v. 3.

the national character. It was shared not only by the pious and the devout, but also by publicans and sinners who, as a rule, did not frequent the Temple or attach any importance to the scrupulous observance of the Law.

So from the beginning we find Jesus much more pre-occupied with the character of God than with His existence. To the question: "What is God like?" He gave a clear and consistent answer from the beginning to the end of His Ministry. At the age of twelve when His distracted parents found Him after an anxious search, He said "Wist ye not that I must be about my Father's business?"[1] And when He died between two thieves, He was heard to whisper "Father, into Thy hands I commend My Spirit."[2]

Would it be true, then, to claim that Jesus was the first in history to call God Father? The answer is "No". In the Old Testament some of the profounder and more sensitive spirits were already groping out towards a more adequate conception of the Divine. One catches a glimpse of it in prophets like Jeremiah and Isaiah, while the Psalmist is wonderfully explicit: "Like as a father pitieth his children, so the Lord pitieth them that fear Him."[3] How then does it come about that we normally associate the belief in the Fatherhood of God with the name of Christ? Are we confronted here with a stubborn myth, one of these unaccountable misreadings of history which simply clamours for correction? The answer again is "No!"

What Jesus did was to take a belief which at best was only dim and spasmodic and fragmentary, and make it central. To Him, Fatherhood was not one truth among many concerning the Nature of God. It was the pivot, the axis, the centre round which everything else revolved. Not for a moment would He deny that God was Creator, Judge and Everlasting King, but first and foremost He was a Father that pitied His children.

[1] Luke 2, v. 49.   [2] Luke 23, v. 46.   [3] Ps. 103, v. 13.

In his book *Jesus, Son of Man,* George S. Duncan writes—" Jesus' proclamation of the Divine Fatherhood is something very different from the enunciation of a general truth that God is the Father of all men and that all men are His Sons. By His preaching and teaching, by His works of mercy and power, by the whole character of His life, Jesus gave to the world a new demonstration of the Divine Fatherhood in action."

We who live in an atomic age are used to hearing that the splitting of the atom marks the end of one era and the beginning of another, and up to a point we can sympathise with those who would argue that this discovery is the supreme revolutionary fact in history. Its possibilities are immense, opening up prospects of unparalleled prosperity. This is undoubtedly true, but far more disturbing and explosive is the revelation of the Divine Fatherhood that was given to mankind in Jesus Christ, and the conviction that has ever since filled the soul of man that behind all the mighty forces of the universe, all the mysteries and tragedies of life, there are at work the loving and wise purposes of a Heavenly Father. The implications of such a belief are incalculable and in the end irresistible. There are certain practical consequences which become increasingly evident as history unfolds itself.

The Fatherhood of God implies, first, the brotherhood of man. History is littered with the debris of experiments in human brotherhood which have come to nought because they did not rest on a solid religious foundation. Perhaps the best known example is the French Revolution. Within one generation disillusioned crusaders learned that the kind of fraternity which is divorced from Fatherhood is not a practical possibility.

Communism is the next most significant political experiment. No one ought to belittle its superb achievements in the realms of economics, education or applied science, but Communism has failed to create the spirit of brotherhood. When not only satellite countries but also Russia itself live under the constant menace of the secret police, it is obvious that the ideology which creates such conditions cannot inspire mutual confidence.

The challenge confronting Christians is how to work out the implications of the Fatherhood of God in a society torn apart by opposing creeds and colliding interests. It is sheer blasphemy to say " I believe in God the Father " and join in the Lord's prayer unless we are prepared to go farther and work together for the removal of all barriers which separate man from man and breed hostility and suspicion.

The real menace to life in the world to-day is not the hydrogen bomb or intercontinental ballistic missiles, or even man-made satellites speeding through space, but the fact of proximity without community. In former ages we could isolate ourselves, our ideas and our interests, but that is no longer possible. The unifying forces that create proximity cannot be stopped because they are in accordance with the Will of God for His children, but the disruptive forces that prevent community must be curbed, otherwise the world must head towards what H. G. Wells calls "ruin and ultimate night ".

One such divisive force is nationalism. In the modern world proximity is no longer an ideal but a fact. Yet the spirit of aggressive selfconscious nationalism is rampart everywhere. It has been suggested by some discerning commentators that what disturbed British and American opinion most when Russia successfully launched its satellite was not the possible military consequences, but the blow it administered to national pride. It is this outlook, even more than the hydrogen bomb which is the real menace to the continued existence of our civilisation.

Racialism is another of these disruptive forces—

racialism again aggravated by the inevitable proximity that has been thrust upon us. All who sincerely believe in God the Father must repudiate racialism not because it is political dynamite but because it is blasphemy against the Holy Ghost. No man can sincerely repeat the Apostles' Creed and at the same time advocate " apartheid."

Then there is too the scandal of class distinction. This is not peculiar to Britain; it is a universal characteristic, but perhaps we British are more guilty of this sin than any other professedly Christian nation. It is impossible to square class consciousness with a belief in the Fatherhood of God. As Christians we must do our utmost to banish this evil thing from our midst with the weapons that lie to hand, such as education and legislation.

The Fatherhood of God implies, second, the sanctity of individual personality. In the first century the social outcasts in Palestine were beneath the contempt of the religious and respectable represented by the Scribes and Pharisees. Jesus shocked his contemporaries by spending more of His time in the company of " publicans and sinners " than in that of the orthodox and socially accepted classes. He sat and talked with the woman of Samaria[1] as if she were a queen. Of Zacchaeus, the despised and detested tax-collector, He said " He also is a son of Abraham ",[2] and to a criminal dying on the cross He said "Verily I say unto thee, To-day thou shalt be with me in Paradise."[3]

Jesus placed a tremendous value on the individual— a fact that we are in danger of forgetting in this collectivist age. The parables of the lost son, the lost coin, and the lost sheep, are all driven home with this truth. In the eyes of God the individual is of infinite value. " He loves us ", says Augustine, " as though there were but one of us to love."

[1]John 4, v. 7.   [2]Luke 19, v. 9.   [3]John 23, v. 43.

Conan Doyle, the creator of Sherlock Holmes, was at
heart a most compassionate man. He went off his sleep
if he felt that any one was suffering undeservedly. At
the height of his reputation as an author and a sports-
man, there occurred an incident which caused a national
sensation. A young Indian solicitor living in this country
was convicted and condemned for animal slashing
though he vehemently protested his innocence. He got
several years hard labour and his professional prospects were ruined for ever. Conan Doyle, reading the
report of the trial had a strange feeling that the man
was innocent and that he was convicted on trumped-up
evidence. He did not know him, but he felt that to
hurt an innocent man was not merely to injure the name
of British Justice, but also to deny God Who was the
Father of all men. So he dropped many of his activities;
he refused lucrative contracts up and down the country;
he engaged in a vast and ever increasing correspondence.
He badgered high-placed officials, put pressure on the
right nerve centres till a re-trial was granted. The
Indian was declared innocent and set free.

And if Conan Doyle, good man though he was, puts
that premium on the individual, how much more does
God the Father! The Cross of Calvary is the measure
of His interest and passionate concern. In *King Lear,*
blind Gloucester says "As flies to wanton boys, are
we to the gods, they kill us for their sport." Very different is the answer and assessment of the New Testament: "For ye are the temple of the living God ",[1]
writes Paul, and John confirms that with words even
more emphatic: "Now are we the sons of God and it
doth not yet appear what we shall be."[2]

The French scholar Muretus, a Protestant exile from
Toulouse, in the seventeenth century, fell seriously ill in
Lombardy, and was taken to a pauper hospital. The

[1]John 3, v. 2.   [2]II Cor. 6, v. 16.

physicians who examined him said among themselves in Latin, never suspecting the sick man knew the language of the learned : "Let us try an experiment with this worthless creature." Whereupon the sick man answered, also in Latin : "Will you call worthless one for whom Christ did not disdain to die?"

The Fatherhood of God implies, third, the assurance of Immortality. This desire has persisted from primitive times right down to our own day. Plato believed in it and the ancient Egyptians put a supply of provisions in the tomb to help the soul on its journey to the next world. And to-day despite the secularising influence of scientific knowledge, it is possible that the vast majority of mankind still believe in survival. We are perhaps familiar with some of the arguments advanced in support of it.

There is the argument of psychical research. Men of the intellectual calibre of F. W. H. Myers, Sir William Crookes, Sir Oliver Lodge and Lord Dowding claim the fact of survival has been established beyond any shadow of doubt. It is no longer a matter of conjecture; it can be demonstrated under conditions of the strictest scientific impartiality.

There is the argument of love. Man does not desire survival merely for himself. To wish to live beyond the allotted span just for the sake of continuing indefinitely would be what Einstein called "ridiculous egotism". No! Man at his best has wanted to live on in order to be reunited with some one he has loved more than life itself. He feels that love, the most real fact in the Universe, is stronger than death.

There is the argument of waste. Scientists assure us that this planet of ours will one day either cool down or burn out, so everything material and spiritual is destined to extinction. Nothing that has been started will ever reach completion or consummation. God, Who began the experiment, has refused to finish it, and is therefore guilty of colossal waste. The human spirit does not readily accept annihilation.

Now let it be admitted that all these arguments are reasonable. They appeal not only to the rational side of our nature, but to our deepest and holiest feelings. They, in themselves, however, are powerless to create the conviction which shouts " O death, where is thy sting? O grave, where is thy victory?"[1] The truth is that immortality cannot be divorced from the most fundamental belief of the Christian faith—the Father-hood of God. This is the ground of our hope and the hidden spring of our confidence. If God is not our Father, arguments, no matter how persuasive, are point-less. If He is, they are irrelevant. If we can say from our hearts, " I believe in God the Father ", we can add in the same breath, " and the Life Everlasting." There are not two separate independent beliefs. The second is a necessary corollary of the first.

[1] I Cor. 15, v. 55.

CHAPTER 12

FACT OF CHRIST

C. S. LEWIS in his book *Surprised by Joy* tells us how he came to be a believing Christian. Ever since he had gone up to Oxford, he had been a pagan, sometimes flirting with notions like the Absolute and Reality in a vain attempt to fill a gnawing vacuum within. There came a day, however, when he felt like a man of snow beginning to melt. The powerful rays of some invisible sun had started a softening up process in the hard core of his unbelief. He could almost hear the drip, drip, and trickle, trickle of his abandoned agnosticism. At length he gave up the unequal struggle and admitted that God was God.

But that was only the first step. For months, perhaps for a whole year, he was a theist pure and simple, not a Christian believing that God, Maker of Heaven and Earth, had become incarnate in Jesus Christ. He went to church because he felt religion demanded some sort of discipline and obedience. But he was not happy. No sooner had he got an answer to one question than he began wrestling with another. Which religion among the host of competing rivals was to claim his allegiance? Where, if anywhere, had all the hints and clues and glimpses of man's spiritual striving found fulfilment? Where, he asked himself, has religion reached its true maturity? Willy-nilly he found himself drawn in the direction of the Incarnation. The leap from atheism to Christianity he describes with stark simplicity : " I was driven to Whipsnade one sunny morning. When I set

out I did not believe that Jesus Christ is the Son of
God, and when I reached the zoo I did."

This very modern man's experience illustrates the inadequacy of a mere belief in God. That is good as far
as it goes, but it is not enough. Inevitably and inescap-
ably comes the question—What sort of God? And once
we ask this we stand face to face with Jesus Christ.

Modern man contents himself at first with a vague
attenuated form of theism. He believes in God after a
fashion, but he is strangely embarrassed by Jesus Christ.
Not that he denies Him in any dogmatic way—that
would demand thought and effort and a certain measure
of sincerity. He prefers rather to shunt Him off into
some unimportant siding of his existence.

The problem is by no means a new one. The Jews
who believed in God with passionate intensity were
mightily embarrassed when Jesus came. To begin with,
they tried to ignore Him, but when that did not succeed,
they crucified Him. How were they to know that they
were pitting themselves, not against a mere man, but
against the incarnate truth of Almighty God. When
men try to stifle the truth, they find themselves convicted by an iron law which decrees that " the stone
which the builders rejected, the same is become the
head of the corner."

When Copernicus, greatly daring, announced that the
earth was not flat, and not the centre of the solar system, men accused him of atheism and blasphemy. In
time, however, his revolutionary theory was universally
accepted, because truth is ultimately indestructible.
There is no need to defend Jesus Christ behind a dogmatic theological line. He is not to be regarded merely
as just one truth among other truths. He is the truth and
the future belongs to Him.

Round about the turn of the twentieth century, certain authors tried to prove that Jesus, as a historical
person, never existed. He was only a figment of the

imagination, a fanciful creation, a mythical figure, giving expression to the religious aspirations of the mere heretical tendencies of the time. These attempts have long since been abandoned and no reputable scholar now gives them a passing thought.

Whatever explanation does justice to Christ, in the end one fact at least is absolutely certain. He is rooted in history. He suffered under Pontius Pilate. No one section of literature, ancient or modern, has been more meticulously sifted or more ruthlessly examined than the Gospels, yet critical analysis has not dissolved Jesus into myth and fancy; rather, He emerges as a real and recognisable figure.

As one would expect, the Evangelists do not all agree on details. Mark's Christ is not in all respects the same as John's. Neither is Luke's Christ the exact replica of Matthew's. But common to each is the basic convention that "never man spake like this man."[1]

Perhaps divergencies in detail should not surprise us. Christ is so big that He breaks the moulds of logical consistency in which men try to encase Him. There are facets of His character which seem glaringly to contradict one another. In His Personality we discern an amazing synthesis of seemingly irreconcilable qualities. There can be no doubt about His tenderness. He took up little children in His arms and blessed them. Yet He could lash out with merciless invective. He was humble beyond compare, living the life of a simple peasant, spurning show and ostentation, yet He made the most staggering claims for Himself. "I am the Light of the world."[2] . . . "I am the Way, the Truth and the Life."[3]

The impact He made on those who were in close contact with Him cannot be measured. The disciples, brought up in strictest Jewish orthodoxy, ardent adherents of monotheism, devout worshippers of a jealous God Who countenanced no other gods, were compelled

[1]John 7, v. 46.　[2]John 8, v. 12.　[3]John 14, v. 6.

to break the First Commandment, and call the Carpenter of Nazareth divine.

The Christ Who is in true fact the author of the New Testament did not stop there. He went on to become the architect of history, without Whose Spirit it is but a grim catalogue of meaningless and disconnected events.

The cynics may sneer at Constantine's decision to make Christianity the official religion of the Roman Empire. They may argue that his was not a genuine conversion but a desperate attempt to save a crumbling Empire from dissolution and death, or that at best it was only a political gesture leaving the morals of the masses largely untouched. That may very well be, but the challenge lies in the fact that Constantine in his dilemma looked to Christianity at all. Who would have predicted such a possibility when Nero and Domitian threw Christians to the lions and forced them underground into the catacombs?

The history of Western civilisation is inexplicable apart from Jesus Christ. When due place is given to the influence of Greek culture, Roman law and administrative genius, His is by far the dominating influence. The Carpenter of Nazareth, denounced by His own people, destroyed by His enemies, has become the Supreme Personality of all time, " the stone which was set at nought of you builders, which is become the head of the corner."[1]

We are conscious of His political influence. The slow agonising growth of the Western world through serfdom, feudalism, absolute monarchy, to a functioning representative democracy, is due to His liberating spirit. Highly significant is this fact that in countries where godless ideologies supplant Christ, tyranny is at once enthroned.

[1]Acts 4, v. 11.

We are aware of the same influence in social reform. It may be true that at times the Church too closely allied itself to the *status quo,* but nevertheless it is impossible to separate social reform from dynamic personalities inspired by the Spirit of Christ. Our hospitals, our education, our factory acts, and the abolition of slavery were all set in motion by men who confessed Christ as Lord, and obeyed Him as Master. Toynbee may talk in eulogistic terms of the higher rival religions, but when it comes to practical humanitarianism they do not stand comparison. C. S. Lewis at one stage of his spiritual pilgrimage was attracted by Hinduism, but abandoned it because of the hiatus between profession and practice—" the Brahmin meditating in the forest, and in the village a few miles away temple prostitution, sati, cruelty, monstrosity."

His impact in the realm of culture is profound. He inspired Leonardo, Michael Angelo, Raphael, in art; Dante, Milton, Browning in poetry; Dickens, Tolstoy, Dostoievsky, in prose; Bach, and Handel, in music. " His Name," said Emerson, " is not so much written as ploughed in history."

It may be possible to ignore the New Testament and to misread history, selecting only these parts of it which lend sanction and support to our own personal bias, but it is difficult all the time to elude the challenge of Christ Incarnate in human character. Stephen was the first Christian martyr. It is highly significant and suggestive that Paul was the young man in charge of his execution. An eye-witness of this brutal death, he must have been struck by the way Stephen died. Why did he not die like a Stoic, steeling himself against the agonising pain, impassive, unmoving? Instead, he died praying for his executioners, with a look of unearthly joy on his face as he gazed heavenward, talking to one Jesus sitting on the Right Hand of God. Such conduct clamoured for an explanation. It was the beginning of a quest which culminated in the dramatic experience of the Damascus road.

A man may not be able to evaluate the New Testament critically, or claim to be sufficiently erudite to cut through the complexities of history and separate the wheat from the chaff, but if he is not totally depraved or spiritually atrophied, he can recognise Christ when he sees Him in the character of good men and women. I may not endorse Schweitzer's theology, but in the selfless sacrifice of this patient gentle doctor of the African jungle, I see Christ. I may not agree with Kagawa's passionate socialism, but in the frail, disease-riddled saint of the slums, glorying in his infirmities, I see Jesus Christ. I may not go all the way with Trevor Huddleston on his crusade against racial segregation, but again, in this high-souled sensitive man fighting his heroic battle, taking "up arms against a sea of troubles", I see Christ Himself. "Verily I say unto you, Inasmuch as ye have done it unto one of the least of these My brethren, ye have done it unto me."[1]

Berdyaev tells us in his autobiography that what brought him to the inner heart of the Christian faith, was not theology or history, nor even the Church, but the self-effacing act of a simple woman called Mother Maria. When the Nazis were liquidating Jews in their gas chambers, one distraught mother refused to part with her baby. The officer in charge was only interested in the correct numerical returns, so Mother Maria without a word, pushed the mother aside and quietly took her place. This act of self-immolation reveals Christ not merely to a thinking philosopher but to all men who are endowed with the merest glimmering of spiritual perception.

Confronted then with the fact of Christ in the New Testament, in history, and more intimately in the lives

[1]Matt. 25, v. 40.

of Christian men and women, we are asked to give our verdict. Such a fact must not be confused with other facts, fixed and static, decreasing in significance as the years roll on. Nor must it be confused with the impersonal facts of science, the laws of motion and thermodynamics for example. To be accurate, what we are dealing with is not a fact which has been, but a Person Who is, and continues to be, world without end. We are asked to come to terms not with something like radium waiting to be discovered by long and patient research, but with some one Who comes to meet us and has already begun the search.

Jesus is invincible. He is also inescapable. We can neither ignore Him nor relegate Him to a position of minor importance in the scheme of things. "The stone which the builders rejected, the same is become the head of the corner."[1]

[1]Matt. 21, v. 42.

CHAPTER 13

TOUGHNESS OF THE CHURCH

THE CHRISTIAN CHURCH has always been the target of bitter hostility. Writers like Celsus in the 2nd century, Voltaire and Gibbon in the 18th, have accused her not merely of intolerance but even of crimes against humanity. Limited then to the brilliant few, this antagonism has now become the prerogative of the inarticulate masses.

The attack comes from every conceivable angle : from the materialists who equate the Church with the entrenched forces of reaction; from the intelligentsia who regard her as an absurd anachronism in an atomic age; from the working classes who see her as the incarnation of the bourgeois mentality. These prevailing attitudes Bertrand Russell succinctly sums up in his essay, " Why I am not a Christian." " You find," he says, " as you look round the world that every single bit of human feeling, every improvement in the criminal law, every step towards the diminution of war, every step towards better treatment of the coloured races, or every mitigation of slavery, every moral progress that has been in the world has been consistently opposed by the organised churches of the world. I say quite deliberately that the Christian religion as organised by the churches has been and still is the principal enemy of moral progress in the world."

This is of course a gross exaggeration. It is more; it is a palpable falsehood and perversion of history, and instances in abundance can be adduced to expose its falseness. But if it contains even a certain measure of truth it might seem to raise the question whether the Church can survive in this new age. This is a question which in a variety of forms has been raised by a number of modern revolutionary thinkers. History has conclusively shown, so these critics allege, that the Church has been weighed in the balance and has been found wanting. It is in process of dissolution and can be ignored as a force to be reckoned with in the shaping of the new world.

Predictions about the decay and early dissolution of the Church are of course no new thing in history. But long ago they were answered in the memorable words of Theodore Beza to King Henry of Navarre, " Sire," said Beza, " it belongs in truth to the Church of God, in the name of Whom I speak, to receive blows, and not to give them, but it will please Your Majesty to remember that the Church is an anvil which has worn out many a hammer."

St. Matthew's gospel, in Chapter 16, throbs with a similar conviction of the indestructible nature of the Church. At Caesarea Philippi on the way to the Cross, Jesus, with a passionate intensity which we feel when we read the words, said " Simon . . . thou art Peter, and upon this rock I will build my church; and the gates of hell shall not prevail against it."[1]

There are New Testament scholars, including T. W. Manson and Rudolph Bultmann, who question the genuineness of these words. They favour the theory that this part of the chapter, the source of so many stormy controversies, is a later accretion. On the other hand the case for the authenticity of the saying continues to receive the support of a large number of scholars of repute—Protestant as well as Roman. Cullmann, in his book on Peter for example, sees no real reason why we should doubt the question. But Cullman would admit that if the passage does represent a genuine

[1] Matt. 16, v. 18.

saying of Jesus, as he himself believes it does, there is still room for question as to the precise meaning and implication. Surely it does not justify the exclusive claims for itself that the Church of Rome has based on it. And one may doubt if it can be taken as strictly applicable to the organised Church as we know her in the world to-day. While this is so, nevertheless it is true that the subsequent facts of history lend strong support to the claim made by Jesus at Caesarea Philippi. Subjected through the centuries to calumny and persecution, the Church has survived the crises and cataclysms of the ages. Her continued existence is not so much a supreme achievement as a veritable miracle. Why has she worn so well? Why has she proved so durable and so resilient in the midst of human vicissitude?

In the first place, the Church was built on a rock of a clear and unequivocal confession. On the very eve of Calvary, Jesus put the supreme question to His disciples—"Whom do men say that I, the Son of Man, am?" They told Him what people were saying—that He was a reincarnation of Jeremiah, Isaiah or John the Baptist. Not content with this answer Jesus pressed—"But whom say ye that I am?"[1] It was then that Peter blurted out the words which form the first statement on record of Christian orthodoxy—"Thou art the Christ, the Son of the Living God."

Jesus, even when he was comparatively unknown, made a tremendous impact on the community. All men discussed Him and speculated wildly as to who He really was. This was no ordinary man, they argued. He defies all normal explanations and leaves us with the task of deciding in what category finally to place Him.

And that question still haunts us. Among my books

[1]Matt. 16, v. 13 l.l.

is one bearing the title *Whom do men say that I am?*
Men as diverse in outlook and temperament as George
Bernard Shaw, H. G. Wells, Charles Darwin and D. H.
Lawrence, all pay tribute to Christ's question, but offer
clashing estimates of His real stature. This confusion
is not confined to the sceptics. We meet it among pro-
fessed leaders of the Church, accredited custodians of
the faith once delivered unto the saints. Bishop Barnes
ends his book *The Rise of Christianity* with the question : " Is the faith centred in the Christ the supreme
expression of religious truth?" The author gives no
answer.

This ambiguity stands diametrically opposed to the
New Testament conclusion : *Christos Kurios*—Christ
is Lord—is the dominant triumphant note of the early
Church. It leaves no room for vague question marks
and conflicting interpretations. To these men Jesus is
not one solution among many. He is the Solver. He
is not one branch of the way, one aspect of the truth,
one expression of life. He is the Way, the Truth, the
Life. The first Apostles did not preach toleration, they
proclaimed rather an all-embracing yet all-exclusive
Gospel. They recognised no rivals. The message they
proclaimed struck one clear uncompromising note. " For
there is none other name under heaven given among
men, whereby we must be saved."[1]

In the second place the Church was built on the
rock of redeemed human nature. " Simon thou art
Peter." Simon was the synonym of weakness and vacilla-
tion; Peter of reliability and rock-like steadfastness. The
man who, unnerved by panic, betrayed his Master the
night preceding the Crucifixion, was the same man who,
after the Resurrection, rallied a tiny band of His be-
wildered comrades and moulded them into the nucleus

[1] Acts 4, v. 12.

of a world Church. The miracle of moral transformation can only be explained by the power of a Risen Living Christ. He took the shifting sands of Peter's character and turned them into granite.

Peter and the other disciples who were the spearhead of a militant conquering Church were converted men. Without aim or motive in life, they were suddenly stopped in their tracks and made to march in a different direction. Renouncing their former allegiances they re-orientated their lives from a new centre. Their universe revolved no longer round self, family, nation or personal ambition. It revolved round the Christ Who had effected in them an absolute transvaluation of values.

But the word " conversion " fills most people with suspicion, if not with hostility. They associate it with the less reputable forms of evangelism which bombard the emotions, bludgeon the finer sensibilities and do violence to personality. They also feel that the effects are so ephemeral and effervescent that the net result is a minus quantity.

We are right to question some expressions of evangelism. Paul certainly did. It would appear that the more strenuously we strive for effect the more transient are the results attained. In practice it seems to work out like a mathematical equation on the inverse ratio principle.

But the outstanding characteristic of New Testament conversion is not effervescence but endurance. It is not something that lightly touches the emotions but a process rooted and grounded in the will. It is not essentially a human decision, though it involves that; it is primarily a divine operation in which God is active all the time. Conversion was not a " flash-in-the-pan " experience for Peter. It lasted from the day he saw the Risen Christ in Jerusalem to the day many years later when he died a martyr in Rome. It stood the test of savage persecution in one of the most turbulent periods of history.

This is the Church's secret weapon. She may unerringly diagnose the modern malaise, master the problem of communication and assimilate contemporary philosophies, but unless, in the name of Christ, she can say to men enslaved by habit and broken by life, "Simon, thou art Peter," the message she proclaims is as useless as a high explosive shell without a fuse.

Arnold Toynbee, in his Gifford Lectures, pays generous tribute to the character of the early Christians. He writes: "The Christian Church won the heart of the masses because it did more for the masses than was done for them by any one of the higher rival religions, or by either the imperial or the municipal authorities, and the Christians were the only people in the Roman Empire, except the professional soldiers, who were prepared to lay down their lives for the sake of an ideal."

In the third place the Church was built on the rock of God's undefeated purpose "and the gates of hell shall not prevail against it." This is not hyperbole, it is history. The last 2000 years have proved beyond any doubt that the birth and growth of the Christian Church was no accident, but the expression and expansion of God's Purpose in the world. What happened in the Graeco-Roman world of the first century defies explaining along humanistic lines. If we approach the phenomenon without bias, we are compelled to cry: "This is the Lord's doing and it is marvellous in our eyes!"

Consider the astonishing universality of the Christian Church. She first saw the light of day in a simple—some would say primitive community—yet she has leapt across national frontiers and geographical limitations. At home in the East, cradle of ancient religions and competing creeds, at home in Europe, birthplace of all we mean by modern culture; at home in America, lead-

hyperbole ≡ gross exaggeration

ing exponent of applied science and technology, she is definitely the Church of the future. How can we explain this except in terms of the Purpose of God?

Or consider her incredible resilience. At times she has been sick unto death, weakened not so much by attacks from without as by apostasy from within. On more than one occasion it looked as if God Himself had abandoned Her. Prior to the Reformation when Popes vied with one another in political intrigue and moral lechery, the outlook was indeed grim. So it was in the sixteenth century when a monk by the name of Tetzel went about selling indulgences at exorbitant prices. So it was in the eighteenth century when an English king complained that more than half of his bishops were atheists, yet the Church recovered to produce men like Luther, John Wesley, Albert Schweitzer, and Kagawa. How can we explain this except in terms of the Purpose of God?

Finally, let us consider Her sheer indestructibility. If we had been in Jerusalem that night when they took a dead Christ down from the Cross, and laid Him in a tomb, how long would we have given the Christian Church? If we had lived when the Emperor Domitian unleased his savage might against Christianity; if we had watched the whole-hearted slaughter, the young Church bleeding to death, and the saints of God crying : " How long? How long?" how many years would you have given Her? A decade at the most perhaps. Yet She has proved more than a match for the whole pantheon of dictators, ancient and modern. How can we explain this astonishing toughness except in terms of the Purpose of God?

The issue, therefore, is piercingly clear. In giving our allegiance to the Church we are supporting not a lost cause but the most permanent institution in history. We are in league not with something local or temporary but with the Power that governs the universe itself. Not even the combined might and subtlety or organised evil will affect the ultimate issue, for on the authority of Christ we know the Church is invincible. She is the most abiding of all institutions, concerning which one can say, " As it was in the beginning, is now, and ever shall be, world without end. Amen."

CHAPTER 14

CHALLENGE OF THE SAINTS

IN BYGONE ages the veneration of the saints became a veritable cult. Their bones " more precious than gold " were preserved as sacred relics to encourage the faithful veterans and to edify those who were still infants in the faith. The early Christians used to celebrate communion over the tombs of the martyrs. They were deliberately held up as an ideal to aim at and an example to emulate.

In time the practice lent itself to abuse and superstition but, on the whole, the instinct which inspired it was sound and healthy. It pointed men away from ordinary human mediocrity to towering peaks of moral grandeur.

Since the Reformation there have been two main streams of tradition regarding the saints. The Roman Catholic Church canonises only a select few who, by dint of superhuman effort and ascetic renunciation, have been deemed fit to qualify. Proof of some miracle associated with the candidate's name, either during his own lifetime or after his death, is required. The Protestant practice is much less defined. Miracles are dispensed with as irrelevant. It sets its face sternly against the cult of the elite and holds that every calling is a priesthood, and that its most menial task is holy.

It is possible that the Church to-day produces as many saints as she has ever done in any previous epoch of her history. They are, however, not so easily recognised nor are they so eagerly venerated. The explanation for this new evaluation is complex, but one reason is that the contemporary mind has fastened on secular substitutes which have won the admiration and called forth the adulation of the masses.

In recent times the scientist has come to occupy a position of pre-eminence. This is not at all surprising for he has become the miracle man of the twentieth century. Edison says "Let there be light", and there is light. Marconi makes the wind, or more correctly the ether waves, his messengers. The Wright brothers fly above the clouds and ride the storm. Nor is the scientist altogether an unworthy object of admiration. Consumed with a passion for truth, he is a living example of single mindedness and dedication.

Of late the athlete has leapt into prominence. The Greeks, it is true, attached great value to athletic prowess, but it is only in the twentieth century that this cult has reached its zenith. So high has the athlete's prestige become that now many countries are prepared to release him from work and pay him handsome sums of money if only he will enhance the national glory. The brilliant footballer, baseball player, runner or boxer, is accorded the admiration once meted out to a major deity in the Greek Panthenon. Nor again is this so mystifying as it may at first appear. The successful athlete has subjected himself to a stern discipline, hence part of his appeal to the applauding crowd.

And there is of course the popular hero. Every known culture has thrown up a crop of them—Odin, in Scandinavian saga; Beowulf in Anglo-Saxon; Hercules in Greek myth, and Cuchullin in Celtic lore. Each generation selects its own particular hero, and the people take him to their hearts. It is no accident that Douglas Bader, during the great World War, became a byword. The courage of a man with both legs amputated, who surmounts such crushing odds to become a great fighting pilot, appeals straight to the human heart.

Courage has always exercised a magnetic pull; it never fails to appeal.

Which raises the question—are these substitutes sufficient in themselves? It is true, as Baron von Hugel pointed out long ago, that every act of heroism and selfless devotion has in it something which is of the very essence of religion. The dedicated scientist, the single minded athlete, the indomitable hero, may indeed be saints-in-the-making, but the Christian Church can never accept them as adequate objects of admiration. The saints cannot be by-passed.

The challenge of the genuine saint is illustrated by the legend which has gathered round the name of the Apostle James. It tells that his accuser was so impressed by the martyr's bearing that, on the spot, he repented and declared his conversion to the new religion. Whereupon he too was condemned and led out to die. When he asked the Apostle's forgiveness, James, after a single moment's hesitation, kissed him and said " Peace be unto thee ". That may be myth, but there is no doubt that the saints have always exercised a mysterious compulsion over the human spirit. They are our best answer to atheism. They refuse to be explained away.

W. T. Stace, Professor of Philosophy at Princeton University, was an agnostic. Convinced that religion, whatever the label, was a concoction of myth and make-believe, and that the experiences of the mystics were explicable in terms of subjective illusion, he wrote and argued eloquently on that theme for many years. Then he took to studying the saints, and the fact that impressed him above all else was neither their compassion nor their unworldliness, but their radiance. It was not that they received preferential treatment from a fond discriminating deity. The evidence went to show that they suffered more than most mortals and sometimes died the most excruciating deaths. Yet through the most harrowing ordeals, their spirits shone bright and clear, defying extinction. This convinced Professor Stace that they were drawing, not on the hidden inner resources we all possess, but on something more ultimate and inexhaustible—God Himself.

What then is it that distinguishes the saint from the good man? We could enumerate any number of virtues like humility, honesty, loyalty, but what really marks him out is the impression he gives of possessing something extra, an ample abundance "good measure, pressed down, shaken together, and running over." This is what T. S. Eliot has in mind when he makes Reilly in *The Cocktail Party* say " The best of a bad job is all any of us make of it, except of course the saints."

This superabundance of vitality expresses itself in a glad contagion of high spirits which the most hardened sceptics have found it difficult to resist.

The saint has experienced the joy of one who has made a great discovery. On every level of human experience, the emergence of an important truth generates an inner glow which cannot be suppressed. So Keats found when first he opened Chapman's Homer :

> Then felt I like some watcher of the skies
> When a new planet swims into his ken.
> Or like stout Cortez when with eagle eye
> He stared at the Pacific . . .

So Madame Curie felt when after the long weary years of experimenting, she saw one night in the darkness of the laboratory the faint phosphorescent blue that was radium. So also did Sir Ronald Ross, on the never-to-be-forgotten day he saw for the first time the relation between malaria and the mosquito insect. Long and laborious had been the agonising quest, but at last he held the secret in his hands. That very night, overcome with joy, he wrote :

This day, relenting, God
Hath placed within my hands
A wondrous thing; and God
be praised! At His Command
Seeking His secret deeds
With tears and toiling breath
I find thy cunning seeds,
O million murdering death.
I know this little thing
A myriad men will save.
O death, where is thy sting?
Thy victory, O Grave?

Neither the raptures of the poet nor the exhilaration of the scientist can be compared with the saints' ecstasy; and because it beggars description and defies language, it can only express itself in joy. " The Christian saint is hilarious " said Tertullian, and no wonder, for has he not seen beyond the temporal to the heart of the Eternal?

Again the saint has experienced the joy of one who exults in a great deliverance. Dostoievsky in his younger days was a revolutionary who denounced the existing order of things. Arrested with a band of fellow-conspirators he was sent to prison. One cold winter morning at dawn along with a number of his shivering companions he was dragged out and made to stand against a wall in front of a firing squad. A priest was summoned to administer the last rites. The prisoners' eyes were bandaged, and in the tense silence, all they could hear was the priming and the cocking of the guns. Suddenly these noises were drowned by the thunder of a galloping horse fast approaching. When it stopped, there was a murmur of voices and after what seemed like an eternity, the prisoners were told that the death sentence had been commuted to one of exile and hard labour in Siberia. So overcome was Dostoievsky with the dramatic suddenness of this deliverance that he sank down to his knees in the snow weeping unrestrainedly.

This is a very inadequate picture of how the saint feels when he knows God by His Grace has delivered him from the bondage of sin and the tyranny of self. " I feel," said Luther, describing his conversion in the reading room of the Augustinian monastery at Wittenberg, " as if I had been wafted through the gates of Paradise." John Wesley is equally vehement about his Aldersgate Street experience. Only a man exulting in new found liberty could write " an assurance was given me that He had taken away my sins, even mine, and saved me from the law of sin and death."

But most of all, the saint experiences the joy of one who exults in the miracle of integration. A good deal of human misery can be traced to the civil war that rages within us. Victims of conflicting impulses and divided loyalties, we would all confess with Paul : " The good that I would I do not, and the evil that I would not, that I do."[1] C. S. Lewis on the eve of his conversion indulged in some introspection. This is how he describes it : " For the first time, I examined myself with a seriously practical purpose. And there I found what appalled me; a zoo of lusts, a bedlam of ambitions, a nursery of fears, a harlem of fondled hatreds. My name was legion."

The more we know ourselves, the plainer it becomes that morally speaking we are schizophrenic. The war within is not merely between spirit and body, it is fought on every front and level of personality. We feel ourselves to be not one but many.

Within my earthly temple there's a crowd,
There's one of us that's humble, one that's proud;
There's one that's broken-hearted for his sins:
There's one who unrepentant, sits and grins,

[1]Romans 7, v. 19.

There's one who loves his neighbour as himself,
And one who cares for nought but fame and pelf.
From much corroding care I should be free,
If once I could determine which is me.

Now the saints, whatever culture they belong to are
one in asserting that only in God can this inner dis-
harmony be resolved. No man can be at peace with his
torn and divided self till first he is reconciled with his
Creator. Only in communion with the Divine can he
experience what Wordsworth calls "the central peace
subsisting at the heart of endless agitation."

But isn't Jesus Christ enough? we ask. Yes, indeed!
"For there is none other name under heaven given
among men whereby we must be saved."[1] But the saint
never elbows Him out of His central position. He only
emphasises it. The Divine Love perfectly revealed in the
Life of Christ is disclosed in a lesser but to a remarkably
luminous degree in others. Many definitions have been
given of what constitutes sainthood, but the one I prefer
above all is this: "A saint is one who by his life on
earth makes it easier to believe that there is a God,
and to wish to draw near to Him."

The saint condemns and comforts at one and the same
time. His purity shows up our own pusillanimous behaviour and induces a sense of shame. He comforts in
that it is in sinful human nature in the tainted stock
of Adam that God has wrought this miracle of grace.
The saint disturbs and haunts and appeals. The effect
he has upon us can perhaps be best described in the
words Iago used of Cassio:

> *He hath a daily beauty in his life*
> *That makes me ugly.*

[1]Acts 4, v. 12.

CHAPTER 15

AUTHORITY OF EXPERIENCE

ORGANISED OPPOSITION to Christianity is stronger than many of us are inclined to think. In China most Christian missionaries have recently been deported; in Russia the Church is allowed to function only if it supports the status quo. In Europe—especially in such countries as France, Italy and Spain—anti-clericalism is rife. Even in the English-speaking nations the spirit of secularism is so strong that it threatens to undermine the foundations of the faith.

Yet as much is to be expected. A nodding acquaintance with the New Testament ought to prepare us. Jesus said : "And ye shall be betrayed both by parents, and brethren, and kinsfolks, and friends; and some of you shall they cause to be put to death. And ye shall be hated of all men for My Name's sake."[1]

The knowledge that iniquity is either openly organised or at work secretly underground should be, by this time, accepted. It has ever been so, and Christianity has always faced up to it. What we ought to find deeply disturbing is the spectacle of a feeble and fumbling institutional Church. I think I know what Middleton Murry is asking when he says : "There are millions of Christians in the world; how do they manage to accomplish so little?"

Religion is intertwined with the fabric of British society. In no other nation is it more inextricably mixed up with political systems and social attitudes, yet according to Sir Sydney Smith, former Professor of Forensic

[1] St. Luke 21, 16 and 17.

Medicine in Edinburgh University, violent crime has been on the increase ever since 1900, and the amount of money we spend on gambling has reached astronomical proportions. Gerald Heard claims that there has been a serious slump in private morals since the turn of this present century. In America, though organised religion is flourishing, its influence on social ethics is disappointing. "Why are the Churches full in America and the local politics to rotten?" asks one outstanding American theologian.

What can the explanation be? Has the Christian faith, long regarded as a leaven in society, lost its yeast-like properties? Has it ceased to ferment? Has it become stale? Has it sunk down into a state of pallid insipidity, murmuring ancient shibboleths and anaemic platitudes? To be sure, the situation is maddeningly complex, defying any facile diagnosis. But, nevertheless, I am convinced that the root cause of our futility is the absence of a first-hand religious experience.

The vast majority of people believe in a theoretical God. Intellectual atheism never had a wide appeal. For the most part it was a rebellion of the mind against the frightful literalism and crass obscurantism of certain brands of orthodoxy. The so-called classic atheists have been unfairly labelled. They may have discarded the mediaeval conception of the Christian God, but they did believe in some principle or power operating behind the perplexing panorama of human existence. This is probably true of men like Gibbon, Voltaire, and Hume in the eighteenth century—the age of scepticism. It is certainly true of T. H. Huxley and Herbert Spencer in the nineteenth, and of Wells, Maugham and Bernard Shaw in the twentieth. The more one reads these authors the more one is struck not by how little but by how much they really believed. The Christian God may have been repudiated, but in His place all sorts of substitutes were thought up—the evolutionary urge, the life force, and the principle of causality.

Nor is all this—abstract as it may sound—divorced from the thinking of the ordinary man in the street. Speak to him of religion and invariably his answer is "I may not believe in the Church but I do believe in something." That this universe should come into existence as a result of mere chance is inconceivable. The very rhythm of nature points beyond itself to some sort of order and coherence. In short, the God most people believe in is an intellectual abstraction, cold and dead and utterly chilling to the human heart.

Napoleon was once crossing the Mediterranean on a clear starry night. Walking on deck he heard a group of his officers hotly arguing the pros and cons of religion. One of them in loud dogmatic tones waved aside belief in God as absurd and antiquated myth; whereupon Napoleon strode up to him, tapped him on the shoulder and pointing a finger at the stars, asked : "Who then made the constellations?"

This dictator who plunged Europe into the abyss of war with all its frightful and inhuman consequences, sincerely believed in the existence of an abstract God. It satisfied his intellect. But such a God, a remote and cosmic abstraction, exercised no influence on his behaviour. It curbed neither his egotism nor moderated his pathological lust for power.

To-day there are no atheists in the Victorian sense of the word. We all believe in some ideology or other, for, as Luther said long ago, "If men have no God they must have an idol." But the value of any creed is seen in the way it affects a man's everyday conduct.

In 1949, in America, a nation-wide poll was taken on religious questions. Asked whether they believed in God, 95% answered "Yes". Asked whether they tried to lead a good life as a result, only 25% admitted any con-

nection between the two. Asked whether religion in any
way affected their politics and their business, 54% said
" No ". The conclusion to be deduced from these statistics is not the irrelevance of religion, but the ineffective-
ness of the theoretical God most people believe in.

Some time ago, I saw on television a professor of
astronomy lecturing on the composition of the universe.
He illustrated it with the aid of ingenious models and
diagrams drawn to scale. One in particular that in-
trigued me was the rings round Saturn. The explanation
the Professor gave of this phenomenon completely satisfied my intellect, but it had no noticeable effect on my
moral behaviour. The theoretical God is exactly like
that. He is as remote and impersonal where normal
conduct is concerned, as the rings round Saturn.

There is also a substantial number of people who
believe in a traditional God. Let us frankly confess
it that Christianity has come down to us by inheritance.
No man is a spiritual Columbus sailing out into the unknown uncharted seas of the soul on his own. What we
know initially about God has come to us through the
media of family, Church and community. The God
Who first spoke to our infant minds and stirred our
early questionings was the traditional God from Whom
we can no more escape than we can escape from ourselves. The truth is, our ego would not be what it is
now, apart from Him. The most thorough-going sceptic
can neither discard nor discredit Him. Our mental
attitudes and our moral reflexes are coloured and conditioned by the pressure of traditional religion. The man
who talks glibly of turning his back on religion is simply
deluding himself. How can he be so naïve? Religion
confronts him in every church spire, in our democratic
institutions and in our code of justice. Professor Joad
was surely right when he said: " Religion is not a

language, something which you acquire; it is bound up with the ancestral elements of your being."

But tradition by itself is not enough. If it were, there would be no need for men like Luther, John Wesley, and Thomas Chalmers. The truth is that under its own steam it gradually slows down and inevitably comes to a dead stop. From time to time it needs to be revitalised by contact with dedicated, dynamic personalities.

John Wesley is the classic example. Here was no pagan plucked as a brand from the burning. Devout and disciplined, to all who knew him he appeared to be the model Christian. Asked if he believed in God, and this paragon of Christian piety would answer with unfeigned astonishment : " Believe in God? He is the mainspring of all my motives, the background of all my thinking, the inspiration of all my dreams. Believe in God? I could not possibly live without Him." So John Wesley believed. Then suddenly tragedy struck him. The Christian community he served in Georgia denounced and disowned him. The girl he loved jilted him. He had to run for his life, and came back to England a broken, bitter, disillusioned man. In the hour of testing the God Whom he had served was found wanting. He longed for something more immediate, and personal and intimate. He needed a God Whom he could call his own, an unfailing source of strength and sustenance and inner peace.

Perhaps in all ages only a minority of people have come to know the God of personal experience.

" O God," cried the psalmist, " Thou art my God."

This is essentially the God of the Bible. I know that in Holy Writ other facets of His Nature are stressed. He is the Judge of all the earth. He is the Lord God Omnipotent. He sitteth on the circle of the earth and the inhabitants thereof are as grasshoppers. He is the Alpha and Omega, a thousand years in His sight are as yesterday. All that is true, but first and foremost He is a personal possession. We neither know Him nor understand Him, nor really believe in Him till we can say "O God, Thou art my God."[1]

There is the God Job discovered in the depths of black despair. "I have heard of Thee by the hearing of the ear: but now mine eye seeth Thee."[2] This is the God that spoke to Elijah crouching in misery at the mouth of the cave. "And after the fire a still small voice, and it was so, when Elijah heard it, that he wrapped his face in his mantle, and went out, and stood."[3] This is the God Whom Isaiah saw with great vision and who compelled him to cry "Here am I, send me!"[4] This is the God Who strengthened Paul on the eve of his execution, moving him to cry "For I know Whom I have believed, and am persuaded that He is able to keep that which I have committed unto Him against that day."[5]

Nor has the sense of first-hand experience weakened in any way with the passing of time. It is not confined to the prophets and apostles of old. Throughout the ages at sundry times and in diverse places the fire of personal conviction has leapt up like a live volcano long thought quiescent. Its glow can be felt even in cold print, and those who recognise it know that faith in the living God is never quite dead. It smoulders under the surface and is liable at any time to erupt with incalculable consequences for mankind.

Pascal was not content with conventional religion. He prayed passionately for a deeper awareness and a more intimate knowledge of God, and one night it came upon him with overwhelming force. The account of this experience, carefully copied on parchment and sewn in the lining of his coat, he carried until the day of his death. This is the record:

[1]Ps. 63, v. 1.   [2]Job 42, v. 5.   [3]I Kings 19, v. 13 and 12.
[4]Isaiah 6 v. 8.   [5]II Timothy, 1, v. 12.

The Year of Grace 1654.
Monday, 23rd November, day of Saint Clement, Pope
and Martyr, and others in the martyrology.
Eve of Saint Chrysostom, Martyr, and Others.
From about half past ten in the evening till about half
past twelve.

Fire.
God of Abraham, God of Isaac, God of Jacob.
Not of the Philosophers and scientists.
Certainty, Certainty, Feeling. Joy. Peace.
God of Jesus Christ.
Deum meum et Deum vestrum.
Thy God shall be my God.
Forgetfulness of the world and of all, except God.
He is to be found only by the ways taught in the Gospel.
Greatness of the human soul.
O Righteous Father, the world hath not known Thee,
but I have known Thee.

This, then, is the authority of experience. Neither
Church nor tradition nor theology can create this inner
certainty for which man secretly longs. We receive it in
a Divine-human encounter, in the experiencing soul
of man, " in that secret place of its life where the Voice
of God is heard."

CHAPTER 16

DEMAND FOR A VERDICT

THERE WAS a time when primitive man believed that our lives were at the mercy of mere chance and caprice, but as the ages passed and he himself progressed, he discovered order and rhythm behind the seeming confusion and contradiction of things. To our fathers, the idea of flying in aeroplanes was as inconceivable as a flight to the planet Mars is to us now. Indeed a few years before the First War a team of experts set up by the British Admiralty dismissed the claims of the Wright Brothers as sheer fantasy. Since then the aeroplane has revolutionised not only the conduct of war but our whole attitude to life. It has obliterated natural boundaries and made the idea of one world a practical proposition. Not so long ago, the scientist pictured the atom as infinitesimally small and ultimately irreducible, but he continued his research and his consequent discoveries seemed to point either to the utter annihilation of the human race or the advent of an era of unparalleled prosperity and peace.

It is not surprising therefore to find twentieth century man laying inordinate emphasis on the importance of free enquiry and disciplined research. It has produced miraculous results. There is no door it cannot open, no secret it cannot unveil. No wonder men have deified reason and hailed it as the saviour come to deliver them from human bondage. Dr. J. H. Oldham is surely right when he says : "The most serious competitor of the Christian Faith in the world to-day is what we may describe as 'salvation through knowledge.' That is the

working religion of men everywhere, the driving force of
the modern world. It is what makes the wheels go round
in Capitalist America as in Western Europe, in the Communist East and in the fermenting continents of Asia and
Africa."

The method of free enquiry has proved wonderfully
successful in every area of human activity except in that
of religion. Here it finds itself as it were confronted by
a curtain of impenetrable darkness. Job, in his famous
cry "Canst thou by searching find out God?"[1] was no
doubt posing a rhetorical question, but he was also
implicitly recognising man's failure to unravel the ultimate mystery.

John Baillie, in his recent book on Revelation, poses
the same problem. "Hearken we ever so diligently, we
are rewarded only with a stony silence. After all, has
not mankind listened attentively enough these thousands
of years? How men have searched for God! How that
old firmament above us has been scanned on starry
nights with all the agony of prayer! How the paths
of logic have been scoured and scoured again, if haply
they might reveal some sign or hint of the divine reality!
And what, we may ask, has been the result but a tense
and oppressive silence? That sphinx in the Egyptian
desert is the true representation of Deity. Upon our
stormy questionings it turns inscrutable, expressionless
face, but no one has ever heard it speak."

This is no academic juggling with ideas. This is a
problem which exercises the mind of the man in the
street. Why does the universe yield so many of its
jealously guarded secrets to man's searching, while the
question that tormented Job long ago is still unanswered?
Here he has made no progress; he is still in the dark.

There can be but two possible explanations. One is, as
Herbert Spencer maintained, that God is unknowable
and that those who claim knowledge of Him are deluded

[1] Job 11, v. 7.

victims of wishful thinking. The other explanation is that the pure intellectual approach to religion is ineffective, and to find a positive answer we must look in another direction, to the intuitive apprehensions of the mystic and the saint.

There are many people who want to believe in God, but confess they walk in darkness. Others have a vague belief in something or other but lack any real sense of inner conviction. Many still believe in the bare existence of some God; they can be described as theists, for they do not possess the full assurance of the Christian faith. They feel something vital is lacking in their lives. Their problem is how to make the leap from mere intellectual assent to personal acceptance.

There are those who approach the problem by way of argument. This method cannot be dismissed altogether for reason plays an important role in religion. A belief which is intellectually indefensible is not likely to appeal to the best minds of a pragmatic and questioning age. Jesus Himself enjoined us to love God, not only with our hearts and souls and strength, but also with our minds.[1] This undoubtedly is true, but argument by itself, no matter how clear and cogent, cannot create that inner certainty which stands at the heart of authentic religion.

This is shown when one examines the classical arguments put forward in support of a belief in God. They are five in number. One argument is that as man entertains notions of perfection, and as perfection presupposes existence, therefore a perfect being must exist. Another thesis is that as every event has a cause, and as the universe is an event it must have a first cause, namely, a Creator. Then there is the argument from design. Just as the play *Hamlet* points to an author that planned and wrote it, so this law-abiding world and the combination of all its parts, point to a planning mind. There is also the moral argument favoured by the philo-

[1] Matt. 22, v. 37; Mark 12, v. 30; Luke 10, v. 27.

sopher, Immanuel Kant. It claims that our sense of
duty, our feeling of right and wrong, our moral sensibilities, are only to be explained by the assumption that
there is a God Who implanted them in our being.
Finally, there is the argument from history. This is
sometimes called the proof *consensus gentium*. It asserts
that belief in God is rooted in human nature and has
persisted through the passing ages. It would be passing
strange if it had no foundation in fact.

Argument may have some sort of negative value in
clearing away the intellectual cobwebs of false and facile
philosophies, but it cannot generate the conviction which
marks the truly religious man. The martyrs did not
go to the stake murmuring well-turned syllogisms. They
were compelled by a faith whose roots sank much deeper
into their nature.

Nor does argument by itself bring to birth a living
faith in the soul of man. In his book *The Summing
Up* Somerset Maugham shows that he is familiar with
all these classical arguments. Not only does he sum-
marise them clearly and concisely, he gives every evidence of understanding them, but according to his own
confession they proved futile. They left him as they
found him, an agnostic.

There are others who approach the problem by way of
authority, but find themselves embarrassed by the dimin-
ished prestige of the Church. In bygone times men
listened with respect to her pronouncements, and were
prepared to accept her discipline, but this no longer
holds. The Church was not consulted when the first
atom bomb was dropped on Hiroshima. Even the sin-
cere Christian is prone to resent any interference on the
part of the institutional Church. He is inclined to agree
with the Philosopher Berdyaev who protests " As a
free thinker I cannot submit to or admit any tutelage
or censorship of my thought."

That is only one side of the picture. There is another

side, which is entirely different. Men weary of the babel of clashing opinions, sick of conflicts and contradictions are clamouring for authority. Finding themselves in danger of sinking in a morass of relative subjectivity, they are searching desperately for some sure foundation on which to plant their feet.

This psychological pressure shows itself in certain trends which are familiar to us all. There is the universal appeal of totalitarianism. It is perhaps not surprising that the inarticulate masses are swept off their feet by the prophets of materialistic philosophy. What is difficult to understand is how distinguished scientists and profound philosophers are able to advocate ideologies which are indefensible in theory and utterly inhuman in practice. The only explanation is that there is a sub-intellectual stratum in their natures which cries out for an absolute and unyielding authority. This doubtless is what led a physicist of the calibre of Klaus Fuchs to become a Communist.

The same thing happens in religion. Men of high integrity like Monsignor Ronald Knox and G. K. Chesterton, weary of seeking, go over to Rome and apparently have no difficulty in accepting the palpably absurd doctrines of the infallibility of the Pope and the physical Assumption of Mary.

Another fact which impels men in the direction of authority is the new prestige of the expert in our midst. Knowledge has become too vast and too complicated for any one man to master, so there has arisen the cult of the specialist who speaks with increasing authority in a constantly narrowing field. As the expert tends to be listened to with respect almost amounting to reverence, it is perhaps not surprising to hear men argue thus : " The scientist has mastered his subject. When he speaks, who are we to question him?" Similarly, the experts of religion, the saints and mystics, have subjected themselves to the necessary discipline, so when they assure us that God is real, we ought to accept their word.

Now there is a sense in which such reasoning has a certain amount of validity. Religion too can boast of its geniuses and experts, Paul, Pascal, St. John of the Cross, to mention only a few. But no matter how authoritatively these men speak, they cannot create the inner conviction which is the breath of a living faith. "Man", said Middleton Murry, "cannot accept certainties, he must discover them. An accepted certainty is not a certainty, a discovered certainty is."

There is only one authentic approach to this problem, and that by way of obedience. In the Bible, faith and obedience are inseparable. Jesus did not look for cleverness in his disciples; He demanded obedience. "Not every one that saith unto me Lord, Lord, shall enter into the kingdom of heaven."[1] "If any man will do His will, he shall know the doctrine."[2] Jesus did not say "Blessed are those who persevere in searching," He said "Blessed are the pure in heart; for they shall see God."[3] In other words, moral obedience is the organ of spiritual knowledge. It is the key that opens the locked door to let the light from another world shine through.

It is true that religious knowledge cannot be isolated completely from other branches of knowledge. It has a rational content but it is unique by virtue of the fact that it is disclosed in the measure in which we are willing to be morally obedient. A scientist may make momentous discoveries while breaking all the commandments. The same is true of artists and poets. Lord Byron wrote immortal verse while leading a riotously immoral life. But faith demands absolute obedience, a surrender of the entire personality.

[1]Matt. 7, v. 21 l.   [2]John 7, v. 17.   [3]Matt. 5, v. 8.

Religion's all or nothing; it's no mere smile
Of contentment; sigh of aspiration, sir—
No quality of the finely tempered clay
Like its whiteness or its lightness; rather stuff
Of the very stuff; life of life, and self of self.

The first parachute jump I made during the War helped me to understand in a new way the meaning of faith. The ground training was very thorough. Nothing was left to chance. Every possible contingency was taken care of. Our instructors demonstrated how a parachute opened and before we were sent up they used a psychological approach to boost our morale. We were gathered together in a large hangar and an expert lectured us on the almost complete safety of the parachute. On a blackboard with the aid of facts, figures, and imposing columns of statistics he proved to us that out of an aggregate of 10,000 jumps, the number of failures amounted to .0001%. He admitted that very occasionally a parachute only partially opened—a roman candle this phenomenon was called, but the chances of it happening to us were a million to one. To the military mind this may have been good psychology, but as I gazed at the faces of my fellow-parachutists, I knew the lecture had misfired. Instead of building up confidence, it induced a certain feeling of disquiet and anxiety. Each man left the hangar half convinced that his first jump would end in a roman candle, and that the only monument to his memory would be this column of .0001% of failure. In reality there was only one way of becoming sure. One had to go up in an aeroplane oneself. In obedience to the command " Go !" a man had to jump out into outer space, and find out for himself whether the parachute really worked.

It is the same with faith. Neither argument nor authority can create the inner personal assurance we want. The mystics and saints have made the dangerous leap of faith, but no matter how unanimous their verdict, we cannot rest on that. There is no such thing as Christianity by proxy. We can never be certain till we make the leap ourselves. Only then will we find the support of the Everlasting Arms.

BIBLIOGRAPHY

CHAPTER 1

Historia Ecclesiastica Gentes Anglorium Book 2. Chap. 13. The
Venerable Bede

Arrow in the Blue Arthur Koestler (Collins-Hamish Hamilton
Ltd.)

The Conduct of Life Lewis Mumford (Secker and Warburg)

Existence and Being Martin Heidegger (Vision Press)

The Courage to Be Paul Tillich (Nisbet)

CHAPTER 2

The Boundaries of Science John Macmurray. Special reference
to Chap. 5 on Psychotherapy. (Faber)

God was in Christ D. M. Baillie. Special reference to Chap. 7,
" Why Atonement? " (Faber)

The Cocktail Party T. S. Eliot (Faber)

The Genius and the Goddess Aldous Huxley (Chatto & Windus)

Between Man and Man Martin Buber (Kegan Paul)

CHAPTER 3

Heart of Midlothian Sir Walter Scott

What I Believe Count Leo Tolstoy

CHAPTER 4

Christianity and the Social Order William Temple (Pelican Series)

William Temple and his Message Canon Baker (Pelican Series)

The Relevance of Christianity Bishop Barry (Nisbet)

Four Quartets T. S. Eliot (Faber)

CHAPTER 5

A Scientist in Russia Eric Ashby (Pelican Series)

The Retreat from Christianity J. V. Langmead Casserley. Chapter 6.
(Longmans)

Dream and Reality Nicholas Berdyaev (Geoffrey Bles)

The Religious Situation Paul Tillich (Thames & Hudson, 1956)

The Age of Anxiety W. H. Auden (Faber)

CHAPTER 6

The Age of Reason Jean Paul Sartre (Hamish Hamilton)

Religion without Revelation Julian Huxley (Parrish)

The Second Coming W. B. Yeats (Macmillan)
Ends and Means Aldous Huxley (Chatto)
Maid in Waiting John Galsworthy (Heinemann)
I and Thou Martin Buber (T. & T. Clark)

CHAPTER 7
The Brothers Karamazov F. M. Dostoievsky (Heinemann)
Dogmatics in Outline Karl Barth (S.C.M. Press)
Our Knowledge of God John Baillie (O.U.P. 1939)

CHAPTER 8
Life of William Temple F. W. Iremonger (O.U.P. 1948)
An Autobiography David Cairns (S.C.M. Press)
The Recovery of Belief C. E. M. Joad (Faber)
God and Evil C. E. M. Joad (Faber)
Theology of the Sacraments D. M. Baillie (Faber & Faber 1957)
The Plague Albert Camus (Hamish Hamilton)
The Struggle for Europe Chester Wilmot (Collins)
The Principles of Psychology William James (Macmillan)

CHAPTER 9
Hard Times Charles Dickens
Babbit Sinclair Lewis (Jonathan Cape)

CHAPTER 10
An Autobiography David Cairns (S.C.M Press)
Christ and the Modern Opportunity Charles Raven (S.C.M. Press)
Your God is too Small J B. Phillips (Epworth Press)
Experience and Interpretation Charles Raven. Second Volume
    Gifford Lectures 1953. (Cambridge Univ. Press)
The Westminster Shorter Catechism

CHAPTER 11
Is God Evident? Gerald Heard (Faber & Faber)
Jesus, Son of Man George S. Duncan (Nisbet & Co., Ltd.)
King Lear William Shakespeare

CHAPTER 12
Surprised by Joy C. S. Lewis (Geoffrey Bles)
Dream and Reality Nicholas Berdyaev (Geoffrey Bles)

CHAPTER 13
Theology of the New Testament Rudolf Bultmann (S.C.M. Press)
Peter: Disciple, Apostle, Martyr Oscar Cullmann (S.C.M. Press)
Whom do men say that I am? Edited by H. Osborne (Faber)

The Rise of Christianity Ernest William Barnes (Longmans)
An Historian's Approach to Religion Arnold Toynbee (O.U.P.)

CHAPTER 14
Selected Letters Baron von Hugel
Religion and the Modern Mind W. T. Stace (Macmillan)
Here I Stand Roland Bainton (Abingdon-Cokesbury Press)
Surprised by Joy C. S. Lewis (Geoffrey Bles)
Journal John Wesley

CHAPTER 15
Pascal and Kierkegaard D. G. M. Patrick (Lutterworth Press)

CHAPTER 16
Life is Commitment J. H. Oldham (S.C.M. Press)
Idea of Revelation in Recent Thought John Baillie (Oxford Univ. Press)
The Summing Up Somerset Maugham (Heinemann)

Other Fontana Religious Books

MERE CHRISTIANITY

C. S. Lewis. Here at a popular price is a revised and amplified edition of C. S. Lewis's three famous books, *Broadcast Talks, Christian Behaviour,* and *Beyond Personality,* brilliantly presenting the author's modern revaluations of Christian apologetics, ethics and theology.

THE SCREWTAPE LETTERS

C. S. Lewis. This witty and profound analysis of Christian strength and weaknesses outlined in the letters of the elderly devil Screwtape to his young nephew, is a classic of religious exposition.

THE PROBLEM OF PAIN

C. S. Lewis. The author gives his views as a layman on the Christian doctrine relating to all aspects of the problem of pain and explains the existence of pain in a Christian world. "It is really a pleasure to be able to praise a book unreservedly and that is just what I can do with this book."
Manchester Guardian

LETTERS TO YOUNG CHURCHES

J. B. Phillips. The author's most famous book, this is more than a mere translation of the Epistles. It has already become a contemporary classic of Biblical interpretation, a valuable guide for all those who in their groping towards a maturer Christian faith, encounter and are perplexed by the vital but difficult Pauline doctrines which constitute the foundation of Christian Theology.

MAKING MEN WHOLE

J. B. Phillips. Undoubtedly one of the author's finest books—a vigorous and searching appraisal of the place of both Christian and non-Christian in the modern world and of their part in God's purpose.

THE GOSPELS IN MODERN ENGLISH

J. B. Phillips. "It is all to the good that we should be given a translation in straightforward English, and Mr. Phillips has a flair for doing this that none of his predecessors in the task seem to have had."
Times Literary Supplement

Fontana books make available, in attractive, readable yet inexpensive editions, the best books, both fiction and non-fiction, of famous contemporary authors. These include books up to 832 pages, complete and unabridged.

If you would like to be kept informed of new and forthcoming titles please apply to your local bookseller or write to:

WILLIAM COLLINS SONS AND CO LTD
144 Cathedral Street, Glasgow, C.4

Other Fontana Religious Books

THE PLAIN MAN LOOKS AT THE BIBLE

William Neil. This book is meant for the plain man who would like to know what to think about the Bible to-day. It deals with the relevance of the Bible and restates its message for the Twentieth Century.

A SHORT BIBLE

Arranged by Austin Farrer. "I welcome this Shorter Bible as a refreshing reminder of the relevance of God's Word to our world."
Fr. Trevor Huddleston, C.R.

ON THE EDGE OF THE PRIMEVAL FOREST

Albert Schweitzer. After renouncing his academic future in Europe to qualify as a doctor, the author whose personality is so vividly reflected in his writing, describes the building and growth of his hospital at the edge of the damp, disease-ridden Equatorial forest of the Belgian Congo.

CHRISTIANITY AND HISTORY

H. Butterfield. With force and profundity the author states his belief that history testifies to Christianity and Christianity interprets history.

THE MEANING OF PAUL FOR TO-DAY

C. H. Dodd. Professor Dodd suggests the place of Paul in the history of religion, he has sought to bring out the permanent significance of the apostle's thought, in modern terms, and in relation to the general interests and problems which occupy the mind of the present generation.

SCIENCE AND CHRISTIAN BELIEF

C. A. Coulson. The author sets out to show that, far from outdating and nullifying traditional Christian beliefs, science is essentially a religious activity, playing its part in the unfolding of the nature and purpose of God.

MORE FROM THE PRIMEVAL FOREST

Albert Schweitzer. An unadorned and poignant account of almost incredible difficulties and achievements, this book is based on reports sent home by Dr. Albert Schweitzer during his second period in Africa from 1924-27.

CHRISTIAN DOCTRINE

J. S. Whale. The author describes and meets the difficulties which the great Christian doctrines raise for us to-day, and shows how the Christian faith understands human history and death.